"Marc Allen gives new life to old wisdom."
— **Virginia Satir, MA, DSS**, author of *The New Peoplemaking*

"A rich and full book...too positive to resist."
— *Mothering* **magazine**

"An example of how Eastern wisdom which evolved centuries ago has a contemporary meaning for the problems of today.... A splendid interface of east and west, old and new, esoteric and practical."
— **Stanley Krippner, PhD**,
professor of psychology at Saybrook University

"Conveys clearly the awesome creative power available to our deep intuitive nature. Every chapter demonstrates wisdom and insight...and is alive and obviously grounded in Marc Allen's personal experience."
— **Ariel Kent, PhD**, founding director,
San Francisco Institute for Transformational Psychologies

"The word *prosper* in its root means 'wholeness.' That is what this book is all about: how to experience wholeness in every phase of one's life. It is filled with a practical mysticism from which we can all benefit as we enter this New Age of enlightenment."
— **Rev. Catherine Ponder**, Unity Church Worldwide

"Written in a practical and delightfully readable style, *Tantra for the West* dispels many of the myths about what tantra is and is not."

— **Susan Campbell, PhD**, author of *Getting Real: Ten Truth Skills You Need to Live an Authentic Life*

"Allen succeeds in conveying a cheerful, conversational tone, and the reader is made to feel good about the work at hand (self-improvement). Material that less-skillful hands might have obscured in cultish vocabulary is made accessible.... Allen makes it clear he won't demand that you give up meat, TV, or alcohol, only that you take a leap. A fun leap, but a leap nevertheless.... A person seeking change in his approach to life would do himself a service by taking a look at *Tantra for the West*."

— *San Diego Tribune*

TANTRA
FOR THE
WEST

Also by the Author

TANTRA
FOR THE
WEST

A Direct Path
to Living the Life
of Your Dreams

REVISED EDITION

MARC ALLEN
Foreword by Shakti Gawain

New World Library
Novato, California

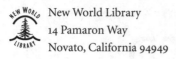 New World Library
14 Pamaron Way
Novato, California 94949

Copyright © 1981, 2015 by Marc Allen

All rights reserved. This book may not be reproduced in whole or in part, stored in a retrieval system, or transmitted in any form or by any means — electronic, mechanical, or other — without written permission from the publisher, except by a reviewer, who may quote brief passages in a review.

Edited by Mimi Kusch
Cover design by Tracy Cunningham
Text design by Tona Pearce Myers

Library of Congress Cataloging-in-Publication Data
Allen, Marc.
Tantra for the West : a direct path to living the life of your dreams / Marc Allen ; foreword by Shakti Gawain. — Revised edition.
    pages   cm
Includes bibliographical references.
ISBN 978-1-60868-342-0 (paperback) — ISBN 978-1-60868-343-7 (ebook)
1. Spiritual life. 2. Self-actualization (Psychology)—Religious aspects. 3. Tantric Buddhism—Miscellanea. I. Title.
BL624.A453 2015
294.3'925—dc23   2015005871

First printing of revised edition, June 2015
ISBN 978-1-60868-342-0
Printed in the USA on 100% postconsumer-waste recycled paper

 New World Library is proud to be a Gold Certified Environmentally Responsible Publisher. Publisher certification awarded by Green Press Initiative. www.greenpressinitiative.org

10   9   8   7   6   5   4   3   2   1

The higher the truth, the simpler it is.

— Abraham Isaac Kook, Jewish thinker, Kabbalist,
and renowned Torah scholar

Dream as if you'll live forever;
live as if you'll die tomorrow.

— James Dean, actor

"What's going on?"
"I'm living the dream."

— A neighbor's reply to my question

Contents

Foreword

When I first met Marc Allen, he had just spent a number of years living and studying at a center of tantric Buddhism run by a respected Tibetan lama. Marc was in the process of trying to integrate the powerful, ancient Eastern teachings of tantra into his life as a modern Western man.

I learned a lot from being around Marc. He was a strong early influence in helping me to discover my own tantric path — a journey that has been unfolding in my life ever since.

This book, written many years ago and now fully revised, contains a wonderful spirit, beautiful insights, and many useful tools.

— Shakti Gawain, author of *Creative Visualization*

In my dreams have secrets been revealed
which our last Dark Age had concealed
But it's still a secret,
only for those who see
Freedom is won only by those
who can dream they're free

Can you hear it, dear Sister?
Can you see it, dear Brother?
It's written large in signs for all to see
So many don't look
So many pass by
And they never really taste being free

— From the song "Sceds" by Marc Allen

Preface to the Revised Edition

The older I get, the simpler I see it, and the clearer it all becomes. Here's one way to sum up the path of *tantra*, the yoga of every moment:

> **Any activity whatsoever, if gone into deeply enough,**
> **leads to ultimate understanding, freedom,**
> **and peace.**

Art can take you immediately into that understanding, but so can every other activity, including meditation and exercising and working and relaxing in nature and cleaning toilets and stepping in dog doo. Every moment, when gone into deeply enough, brings us to the great understanding of the miracle of *what is*.

Music can easily and effortlessly take you there. When playing music, when listening to music, you're in the moment, and the music is telling you that within this moment is the magic, the wonder and joy, of life itself.

Acting, too, if you go into it deeply enough, is a path to deep understanding. You realize that we have all these different centers of energy within our bodies, and we place our essential life energy in different parts of our bodies at different times: Romeo goes from the loving energy of the heart to the anger of the third chakra, his Mars energy. And that anger causes the tragedy.

You can learn through acting — as well as through life in general — that being in different centers of energy is something you can carry into daily life. You can become aware of where your physical, emotional, and mental energies are located. When we focus on a particular energy center, we become fully aware of it, and that awareness itself can cleanse it and purify it and bring out its purpose and strength. In the process, we lighten up all our other energy centers, from lowest to highest, root to crown, grounded in the earth and shining all the way throughout our bodies, all part of the wonder of what is.

Whatever path you choose, it is your path to spiritual discovery, wandering wherever it may take you. It is the path of cleaning up messes, doing the dirty work, watching TV, playing with your electronic devices, eating pizza, and whatever else you are doing at the moment.

Every moment is our path, and any activity whatsoever, if gone into deeply enough, leads to ultimate understanding, freedom, and peace.

So be it. So it is!

Who seeks for heaven alone to save their soul
May keep the path, but will not reach the goal
While those who walk in love may wander far
Yet God will bring them where the blessed are.

— Henry Van Dyke, *The Other Wise Man*

Introduction

Every one of us is absolutely unique, and every one of us is on a journey of personal evolution. It is the nature of all life-forms to grow and evolve, and we are no exception.

Each one of us is evolving in our own way — some of us are very disciplined, and some of us have no concept of or interest in discipline and would rather drink beer and watch TV than do an hour of yoga or meditation.

This book offers a perspective, a way of looking at ourselves and our world, that can have surprising results in our lives. There is an ancient and wonderful way of seeing ourselves that is completely supportive of every one of us and every lifestyle choice we have made. We can learn to see ourselves in this way by simply realizing that we can look at every moment of our lives as our spiritual practice. Once we start practicing every moment, we unleash a process that allows us to make quantum leaps, quickly. We are on a direct path to freedom and awakening and fulfillment in life.

The form of this book is intentionally brief, covering a lot of ground. Its intent is to show you that, always and in every area of your life, the answers are within you — not anywhere else, in any book or anyone else's teachings.

Within your way of life,
within your everyday thoughts and feelings,
within your fantasies and your dreams
are the keys to love, freedom, fulfillment, and enlightenment.

Please read this book slowly. Don't plow through it once, rapidly, intellectually, and think you have absorbed it all. Don't turn it into a race to finish. You don't have to read the whole book, you don't have to read much of it at all, before — if you're open to it — some magic starts happening in your life. So take your time.... Take time to pause at the dots, and take a breath.... Take time to do some of the practices and go through some of the processes. Put the book down every once in a while and reflect on whatever words you find resonating in your creative mind.

You don't need to start at the beginning. Flip through it, open it at random. Wherever your eyes land is exactly what the Universe wants you to see at this moment.

Try a few of these practices with an open mind, and I promise you'll see some wonderful, powerful, sweet, satisfying results in your life.

1

The Direct Path of Tantra

**Open up to the possibility
that there is a quick, direct path in front of you
to the fulfillment of your dreams.**

It's fascinating that when the word *tantra* is used in the West, it's almost always thought of as sex, with some kind of mysticism thrown in. But if you look at how tantra has been taught and studied in the East for the past several thousand years — particularly in India and Tibet — you get a much broader sense of its meaning.

Tantra is not just "the yoga of sex"; it is the yoga of *everything* — of every moment. *Yoga* means "union," so a good way to define *tantra* is "union with everything" or "the practice of every moment." Here's another good definition:

**Tantra is the awareness that every moment
is a direct path to love, freedom,
fulfillment, and enlightenment.**

Tantra is a path, a means, to freedom and fulfillment. What do *freedom* and *fulfillment* mean? It is up to you, of course, to discover what they mean for you — no one can do it for you. Once you can clearly define what freedom and fulfillment mean for you, you can realize them in your life — and it's not all that complex or difficult. Freedom is being free to be yourself. Fulfillment is finding the direct way to realize your greatest, most wonderful dreams.

Tantra is wide open, with infinite possibilities — like life is, and like you are. Tantra includes sex, yet it includes everything else, too — every moment of your life. Every moment is sacred. Every moment is either something to enjoy and celebrate or something to be used as a teaching, a piece of valuable instruction, a message from the Universe for you in your emotional, mental, and spiritual growth.

Everything you are doing, have done, and will do are part of your practice of tantra. Through an awareness of tantra, we discover the unique perfection of every moment of our lives.

You don't have to believe this; you don't have to believe anything that follows. Just read with an open mind, try some of the practices and processes, and see what happens.

This book contains powerful tools that can help you find happiness, love, freedom, inner peace, abundance, power, enjoyment, fulfillment, enlightenment — *whatever your heart desires.* But these tools must be applied, not just read. Understanding intellectually is a very different thing from experiencing deeply, with your whole being. Mental understanding has no effect at all on the quality of your daily life, while experiencing deeply can work miracles.

You can work miracles in your life by spending some time with the principles and practices that follow. All you have to do is open up to them. Open up to the possibility that there is a quick, direct path in front of you to the fulfillment of your dreams. It is up to you.

The Brilliant Concept of Tantra

The concept of and the vast body of teachings encompassed by the word *tantra* are far more ancient than any scholar or historian could ever trace. The word comes from the ancient Sanskrit root word meaning "to weave." Tantra is the stuff of life, the unique fabric of our lives that we have woven over the years.

Tantra has come to us through two vast, multifaceted traditions: Hinduism and Buddhism. Both originated in India, in all likelihood, although Buddhist tantra comes to us through the Tibetan culture. (If you're interested, see the addendum, "Tantra in the East," for more historical details.)

Although every form of tantra is unique, some important points can be made about all tantra:

Tantra is a way of life that involves acceptance of all life. It does not reject anyone or any spiritual path or psychological area of study. It embraces the whole of life. Everything has its own perfect reason for being.

Tantra shows that within every moment of our lives — within every feeling and thought and activity — there are deep and powerful truths that, when examined in a clear light, can lead to making great leaps along our paths in a very short time.

Tantra teaches respect for the individual, recognizing that everyone must evolve in her or his own way. There is no one answer. There is no pat system that will work for everyone. There is only endless evolution, and we're part of the process, whether or not we're aware of it. Simply becoming aware is the most important thing we can do to speed up the process and move into a state of being in which we are peaceful and free.

The Western world is ripe for the ideas and practices of tantra. Westerners are usually too individualistic and too worldly-wise (and a lot of us are way too lazy) to accept most forms of Eastern thought and practice, mainly because they contain a great many of the cultural trappings from the countries of origin. Many Eastern traditions encourage Westerners to go without sex, alcohol, coffee, meat, and "impure" foods; to live a life of rigorous discipline; and to reject a great deal of the culture, heritage, and lifestyles of the West.

A study of the history of tantra reveals that its power, its ability to adapt so successfully to other cultures, rests on the fact that it does not reject modern culture. We don't have to give up sex and meat and TV in order to achieve freedom and happiness. This is the effectiveness and power of tantra. We can create our lives exactly as we want them to be. It is up to us.

Three Different Paths

There is a season for everything, a time for every path. The path of tantra is not for everyone, by any means — only for those wanting something direct and immediate and for those ready to take a leap.

A Tibetan lama living in America told me the following short parable. It is a traditional Tibetan story, and it places the different paths into a simple, clear perspective, while defining tantra beautifully:

There is a path going through the woods. A dense patch of poisonous plants is growing by the side of the path and, in one place, totally engulfs the path.

A monk — with shaved head, robes, and begging bowl — comes up the path. The monk sees the poison and immediately turns around and heads the other way.

Then a bodhisattva — an awakening being working for the enlightenment of all beings — comes up the path. Seeing no way around the poisonous plants, the bodhisattva courageously plows directly through them and keeps moving on up the path.

Finally, a tantric yogi comes wandering up the path. This person has no outward signs of a spiritual life, unlike the monk or the bodhisattva. The follower of tantra sees the poison and plunges directly into the center of it, even though it seemingly takes him or her off the path.

The key to understanding this story also enables us to discover the value of tantra in our lives: The key is that the poisonous plants represent the so-called negative or separating emotions — fear, anger, greed, jealousy, and so on. (Interestingly enough, the Tibetan word for *poison* is the same as the word for *negative emotion*.) This little story presents a clear picture of three alternative reactions to our feelings: We can run from them, we can plow through them as quickly as possible, or we can jump into them and experience them fully.

None of these three choices is any better than the others — each person in the story just did what he or she had to do, and each choice must be respected. It is perfect for monks in some traditions to withdraw from the world, and even to ignore or annihilate their feelings. It is perfect for some people to avoid talking of negative feelings or death, and to put on a happy face — we all do what we need to do on the level of evolution we have attained. But it is also good to be aware that if you choose not to examine your feelings, you might continue to be motivated by fear, and that fear will never lead you to the blessed land of peace.

It is perfect for spiritual seekers to plow through their negative feelings quickly and continue up the path of their (vitally important) work in the world. Most people consider their negative feelings things to be dealt with as quickly as possible in order to get into a more loving, supportive frame of mind.

Are tantric yogis more or less evolved as they plunge into the poison of their negative feelings? It is impossible to say one way or the other. But one thing we know for sure — by using this method, they will evolve faster, by leaps and bounds, than they would by using any of the methods that lead us to avoid or minimize our so-called negative feelings. For one of the most important things to realize about our negative feelings is that until we openly look at, clearly understand, and deal with them effectively, they will retain their power and keep resurfacing over and over again.

The path of tantra is the path of leaping into the fire of our feelings. It is a path of tremendous power and true freedom. It means acknowledging our feelings at every moment — something that children are natural masters of, before they are taught to give up their freedom and sit for six hours a day in a classroom, exercising their rational minds, burying their intuitive visions, and suppressing their feelings.

The Tibetan teacher who told me the story of the three paths emphasized that the path of tantra was a direct path to enlightenment. By going off the straight-and-narrow path toward your goal and plunging into the poison of your negative emotions, you see those emotions for what they are — completely empty at their core — and you discover that you are a being of lightness and wonder.

Confronting Negative Feelings

When we acknowledge and even confront our negative feelings, we are plunging right into the heart of tantric practice. That's our meditation. And that's what I'm inviting you to do — right now, right at the start of this book, the start of this journey into tantra.

I can sense some of you thinking, "Wait a minute! I thought tantra was entirely different. I thought it was going to be fun and exciting!" Well, I can promise you that it will become fun and exciting — but we have some homework to do first, some inner work that is given to us whenever we create a situation in our lives that is not fun or exciting.

Many people don't dare confront their negative feelings, because they feel they would hurt somebody or be destructive in some way if they did. One man at a seminar once went so far as to say that, if he plunged into his feelings, he might rape hundreds of women and kill hundreds of men! But there are *skillful* ways to get into your feelings — ways that don't hurt others, or yourself. Many of the practices and processes that follow deal with these methods.

So many people are afraid of their anger, and this keeps them from confronting and expressing it. But then they end up carrying their anger around with them for years and years. It ends up damaging their bodies, and often their relationships, because it comes out in all kinds of covert ways, such as irritation, anxiety, stress, and periods of deadened silence.

By expressing that anger, you can let go of it. But you don't have to attack anyone to express it. Here are two good methods for getting something off your chest: (1) Let yourself yell and rant and rave and condemn and say all kinds of terrible things when you're driving in your car alone. (2) Go into your room alone and put a pillow on your bed and pretend that pillow is the person you're angry with. Then proceed to yell at it all you wish and pound it with as much physical energy as you care to put into it. Pound it to shreds, if necessary, to blow off steam. You can even use a plastic bat if you wish. (Somehow, something about smashing a pillow with a plastic bat makes it all kind of fun — even a bit funny.)

If you allow yourself to really act out your anger in ways that don't hurt anyone, you'll notice afterward that you feel much better, lighter, relieved. You have found a way to effectively let go of your anger, and you aren't carrying it around with you anymore. If it comes up again, use these methods again, and again if necessary.

Whenever you're in an unpleasant place, confronting a negative emotion, remember: It is not the situation itself that is causing you your problem — it is your rejection of the situation that is causing the problem. Another way to put it is:

It is not the world causing your problems,
it is your own mind,
your resistance to what is.

Don't reject the situations you're in, and don't reject your feelings. Instead, be with your feelings, respect them, examine them. Look closely, and gently, at them. Simply look at what you're telling yourself, and see the thoughts that are going through your mind. Look at them honestly, openly, and as objectively as possible.

The most difficult moments of your life are your finest sources of instruction. These are the times when you can make the greatest leaps forward on your path. Your feelings are a storehouse of wisdom, if you embrace them, and look closely at them.

Within our darkest moments,
our brightest treasures can be found.

You may be wondering what kind of wisdom can come from being angry or jealous or guilty. Look at it this way: There's always a reason for your feelings, often a very simple reason. But when you're caught up in those emotions, you can't see why you're creating them. If you can take a breath and ask yourself why you're feeling the way you are, you learn things about yourself that you've never seen quite so clearly and never been able to express in such simple language. That knowledge alone produces some very positive changes in your life — changes that free you in a great many ways. The process that follows, a tantric practice, provides specific instructions in how to do this.

This may seem like a time of indecision...or confusion...or regret...or pain...or anger. But look again — and this time, don't reject your feelings but embrace them instead. Welcome them, even act them out (as long as you don't hurt anyone else). Discover what you're telling yourself, even if it sounds stupid, or violent, or unloving, or totally negative. By simply taking a clear look at these hidden feelings, you are shining the light of your understanding on them, and you come to see exactly where you are limiting yourself, holding yourself back, being far less expansive, less wonderful, less creative than you really are.

Many so-called negative feelings simply dissolve when looked at in the clear light of an accepting, open mind. Others require more powerful techniques, which we'll explore later on in this book.

As soon as you decide to look into the path of tantra, it becomes obvious that every "negative" feeling you have contains within it an opportunity for growth — if you allow yourself to plunge into it and discover what it is. Every feeling contains within it the understanding, knowledge, and wisdom that lead to true freedom and peace of mind.

If Buddha — the historical Buddha who revolutionized religion and philosophy in India 2,500 years ago — hadn't gone into a period of deep depression and anxiety, propelled into despair by fears of sickness, old age, and death, he never would have begun his years of searching and examining. And he never would have become a Buddha, a "fully awakened one."

Within our darkest moments, our brightest treasures can be found.

A Tantric Practice

This first practice may come as a surprise to some of you, for it doesn't deal with the usual things associated with "tantric practices." But you'll see that it is truly a tantric practice in the broadest, most meaningful use of the word. It is designed to give you insight into yourself.

This four-step practice is best done when you are feeling uncomfortable, emotionally upset, pressuring yourself to make

a decision, or any time you wish to get more deeply in touch
with what's going on in your active mind and body. This little process gets to the essence of the meaning of tantra, for it
reminds us that our state of mind at any given moment is the
perfect teaching for us. Asking the simple questions below will
help to clarify the teaching that is within every one of our feelings. It can help us break through the emotions that seem to
be controlling us and give us the power to master them, and
ourselves.

Don't skip over any of these steps — especially the ones that
may seem insignificant.

1. Ask yourself a question that examines and confronts
    the feelings you're experiencing at the moment. It could
    be, "What am I telling myself right now?" or "What is
    the truth for me about this situation?" or even "What
    am I feeling right now?"

2. Answer yourself with the very first words that come
    into your mind, without censoring anything.

3. Acknowledge yourself, each time you answer, by say-
    ing, "Thank you!" to yourself for sharing these feel-
    ings. Then repeat these steps again, and again — until
    you arrive at an answer that sheds the light of clear
    understanding on your situation. You'll know when it
    happens because you will suddenly feel better, clearer,

more aware of your feelings and attitudes, and more aware of your options.

4. Share your discovery with someone else, within a day or two. This helps to finalize the whole process.

This practice is so simple — yet so powerful! It brings to the surface all the feelings we experience on such deep levels that we don't usually examine them all that closely. Once those feelings surface, and we simply look at them with our conscious awareness, they lose their power.

Yet if we reject them, we continue to give them power to run our lives. The reason this happens is that we're conditioned into a false belief that these feelings are real and powerful, when in reality they're empty, like everything else in the universe, and have no power to affect us. Accept your feelings, say "Thank you!" to yourself for expressing them, and look at them in the light of your conscious mind. The simple act of accepting our feelings works miracles. The simple steps of this process allow us to get into the truth of what we're feeling.

Try this little practice the next time you're upset or dealing with a problem that seems impossible to resolve. Keep doing it, and you'll find yourself dissolving the problem at its roots. And you'll discover the true meaning of *tantra*.

A Message to Myself

Don't reject the sadness
Don't reject the sorrow
Don't reject the suffering
    and the pain
Blessed are these things
For through them we grow
Into true understanding
    of our way.

2

The Power of Affirmations

**Affirmations in some mysterious and powerful way
summon the forces of creation into our lives.**

The practice we just saw involves confronting and accepting
our emotional states, openly and honestly. In so many cases,
that's all we need to do. In other cases, we have to use other
methods to teach ourselves to be free. Engaging the power of
the spoken word through affirmations and mantras (and songs,
poems, and prayers) is one of the simplest and most powerful
ways to change the quality of our lives and create the things we
want in our lives.

The power of affirmations can be stated very simply: *Affirmations in some mysterious and powerful way summon the forces
of creation into our lives.* After all, as it is written so clearly in
the Bible,

"In the beginning was the Word."

To affirm means "to make firm." An affirmation is simply a spoken or written statement, in the present tense, declaring that a desired reality is now coming into being. There is a great mystery about how affirmations work — but fortunately we don't need to understand how they work to set their power in motion in our lives.

We have been making affirmations all our lives. And others have been giving us affirmations all our lives as well, but we haven't been consciously aware of the process and power of affirmations, and so we have affirmed a lot of things that we could do better without.

Anything you say or think to yourself is an affirmation of some kind, for good or for ill. Anything anyone else says to you can be an affirmation, if you accept it as being true for you. Our subconscious mind accepts it all — whether for better or worse. Most of us grew up in environments that weren't totally supportive; most of us had parents, families, friends, and other people in our lives who gave us a lot of terrible affirmations that were destructive to our self-image and our views of the world in some ways. Children all too often tell each other that they're stupid or ugly or unable to do something. Brothers and sisters often say negative, unflattering things to each other. These are unfortunate, negative affirmations.

Most people are still carrying with them, in their basic underlying beliefs, the unsupportive things that people told them when they were so young that they didn't have the awareness to question or ignore them. And these negative affirmations have an especially powerful effect when there's a strong emotion behind them — those moments when Mommy or Daddy is deeply upset and yells, "You never do anything for me!" give the child a deep affirmation of his or her own selfishness or worthlessness.

It's no wonder that people have affirmed themselves into neurosis, depression, poverty, selfishness, sickness, weak and limited self-images, anger, frustration, violence, fear, and so on. Fortunately, affirmations are so powerful that a few minutes of conscious, deep, positive ones repeated daily for a few weeks can undo years of unconscious, deep, negative ones. This is especially true because of this fact:

Positive affirmations have the greatest power
in the universe behind them:
the power of truth.

Because the truth is that you *are* capable of transcending self-imposed limitations; the truth is you have a miraculous physical body, a phenomenal mind, and a connection with a subconscious mind that knows no limits. Your life is not only worthwhile; it is the realization of endlessly powerful forces of creation. And you are loving and compassionate — even though that love and compassion may be buried under years of unexpressed anger and fear and frustration.

Affirm what you know to be true in your heart, and you will create that reality. Affirm that you are free, and strong, and attractive, and prosperous, and loving — and you will find, often in a remarkably short time, that your outer world will begin to change as a reflection of your changing inner consciousness.

The Act of Creation

To understand an affirmation's power to create something, it's good to first attempt to understand how creation works. A great many different mythologies, mystical traditions, scientific studies, and religions have endlessly investigated the mysteries of creation. Many of them have come up with similar findings. The winding path of tantra embraces all these different traditions and worldviews.

The Kabbala — a mystical branch of Judaism — expresses it as clearly and simply as it can ever be stated. Those who have studied other traditions will see many similarities, and those with a scientific approach might see how it helps to explain something about the mysteries of creation.

To study Kabbala is to study the Tree of Life. All things are contained within the Tree of Life, and the creation of the Tree of Life reflects the mysteries of all creation. The study of the Tree of Life sheds the light of our understanding on the mysteries of ourselves, for we are a microcosm, mirroring the vast macrocosm of the universe: As above, so below.

The source of the Tree of Life is in emptiness, in the vast void of space. Then it all begins, first as a very subtle spiritual impulse — the impulse to create within the mind of God, if you will, or within the mysterious intelligence of the vastness of the universe. Then this very subtle spiritual impulse becomes something more tangible: a *thought*, a clearer, more definite impulse to create something. Once the impulse has become a thought, it gains momentum and then becomes a *feeling*, an emotional impulse. This feeling, supported by a sustained thought, *soon becomes manifest in physical form*, as an object we can experience with our senses.

The way in which the Tree of Life is created reflects the way in which everything in our lives is created. Everything has gone through this cycle: It is first a spiritual impulse, then a thought, and then a feeling, and then it becomes a physical manifestation. Think about it: Everything we have created in our lives was first a thought, and then a feeling. Anything we consistently hold in our minds to be true or real will become true or real in our physical universe.

This explains why affirmations are so powerful. They are our very thoughts themselves, supported by our emotions. We are thinking and saying affirmations all the time — whether consciously or unconsciously. The Universe always says *Yes* to our affirmations, always supports them, because we are the Universe, we are the Tree of Life, and we are creating our own reality, through our thoughts and feelings and spiritual impulses.

The Power of Your Words

We are continually giving our bodies operating instructions through our thoughts and words. Simply by being observant, we can become aware of this process.

Everything, before it is created on the physical plane, is at first a thought, then a feeling. Before we can build a house, there must be a blueprint for it, a design, an *idea*. Words are creative ideas spoken, made manifest into the world.

Many people are unconscious of this, often saying things like, "This is making me sick" or "This job is killing me" or "This is really hard; I can't do it." These words are affirmations, words with power. No wonder these people are getting sick, dying too young at jobs they hate, getting headaches, and failing.

Look at your life — clearly and honestly. You'll see what you have been affirming to yourself. Most of us have created a lot of things we would prefer to do without. It is time to consciously affirm that we are now creating something better for ourselves. Here's one simple yet powerful affirmation:

Every day, in every way,
I am getting better and better.

Repeat it to yourself often, and feel it affect every cell of your body.

How to Do Affirmations

Every thought and every word — positive or negative — is an affirmation, and is creating the reality of the affirmation. The simplest way to do affirmations consciously is just to say them to yourself, either out loud or silently, whenever you feel like it. Say them especially to counteract any negative thoughts or words you find yourself thinking or saying.

This is not a tool for repression: Allow yourself to have any thoughts and feelings that arise — don't reject them — and yet give yourself the time and energy to affirm a more desirable reality after those negative thoughts and feelings have come up.

For example, if you find yourself thinking, "This job is making me sick," look at what you're thinking, and see if that's something you really want to create for yourself. If it isn't, affirm to yourself, out loud or silently, *"I am strong and healthy when I do my work"* or *"I am in perfect health, physically, mentally, emotionally, and spiritually"* or *"Every day, in every way, I am getting better and better,"* or something else that feels good to you. Say it repeatedly, if necessary, and say it with emotion, until it feels like it has sunk in. Try to remember to say it every time that old negative thought or feeling arises.

Just by becoming more aware of what you are thinking and saying, you will find that you have plenty of material to deal with. Notice the things that aren't working in your life, and find the right affirmations to correct the situations.

Of course, your feelings about your job may be a very valid reason for you to find another, healthier job. But if you choose to remain in the same situation for now, then create the most positive thoughts you can about it. Replace those thoughts and fears of sickness with thoughts and hopes that every day, in every way, you're getting better and better.

Make affirmations in the present tense, and play with the wording until you find something that is believable to you. Don't affirm, "I am going to create abundance in my life," because the results will always be waiting to happen in the future. Instead, affirm something like, *"I am now creating abundance in my life!"* — and you'll soon find that it is true. Our subconscious mind has no problem accepting that you are now on your way to creating abundance; for me personally, at least, that's a far better affirmation than "I now have abundance," because both your conscious and subconscious mind can quickly make the case that it's not true if you happen to be struggling to pay the rent.

How soon a wonderful level of abundance will come into your life depends on how often you repeat your affirmation and on how strongly you are affirming the opposite on deeper levels of your consciousness. Affirmations are powerful enough to change subconscious negative beliefs into powerful, expansive beliefs. You are not weak and alone and incapable.

**You are powerful, connected to all,
and capable of creating what your heart desires.**

Affirmations in Meditation

Another powerful way to do affirmations is in the relaxed state of mind and body that is often called meditation. When you meditate for even a short amount of time — even just a minute — you see powerful results in your life.

Here's a little practice that is relaxing, energizing, and healthful — and it's also a simple and easy way to deeply absorb affirmations. It's certainly one of the most effective ways there are to create whatever you consistently desire and wish for in your life.

Sit or lie down comfortably. Take a few deep cleansing breaths — even take a few minutes to breathe deeply, if you feel like it.

**Deep breathing is one of the best possible things
we can do for our minds, bodies, and spirits.**

Close your eyes, take a deep breath, and affirm silently to yourself as you exhale, *My body is now relaxing.* Take another breath and affirm, as you exhale, *My mind is relaxing, I am letting go of all thought.* Take one more deep breath and affirm as you exhale, *I am letting everything go.*

Then choose any affirmation — any instructions you want to give your body and mind, anything you wish to create. See it happening here and now as you say your affirmation. If excitement and enthusiasm arise to support the affirmation, all the better — the stronger the feeling, the sooner the reality you wish to create will manifest.

Say your affirmation repeatedly, for as long as you wish. Try these, and see how they feel. Then come up with your own by changing some of the words in these affirmations or by coming up with your own completely different words:

I am deeply relaxed....
I am strong and healthy....
I am open, I am free....

Feel yourself relaxing. See yourself strong and healthy. Feel yourself open and free.

Everything I need is coming to me, easily and effortlessly....

*In an easy and relaxed manner, a healthy and positive
way, in its own perfect time, for the highest good of
all I pray....*

Then list your dreams. Dare to dream your ideal.

*Spirit flows through me every moment with its healing
energy....*
I am guided by Spirit, doing God's will....
*I am now taking a quantum leap in my success in the
world....*
*My marriage and family life are filled with grace, love,
ease, and lightness....*

Choose any other affirmation that appeals to you,
and repeat it, many times, until you feel sure your
subconscious has gotten the message. Picture yourself having completely fulfilled the vision contained
within the affirmation. Enjoy yourself — don't work
too hard at this. Have fun with your creative imagination.

Take a final, deep breath at the end of your session and
affirm:

**This, or something better, is now manifesting,
in totally satisfying and harmonious ways,
for the highest good of all.
So be it. So it is.**

Now return to your waking day, fully relaxed and refreshed, able to easily and effortlessly accomplish whatever you want.

The more energy you put into your affirmations, the sooner
you will experience results. Imagine yourself easily and effortlessly becoming what you are affirming. Don't worry if you can't
exactly visualize it in your mind's eye — just feel it or imagine it
in any way you can. It's such a simple thing to do, and by doing it,
you are creating a new reality in your thoughts and in your emotions. Soon a vast, deep reservoir of power in you — the power
of your subconscious mind, your connection with the infinite —
will bring about in physical reality what you are affirming.

That's worth repeating, and affirming:

**A vast, deep reservoir of power in me —
the power of my subconscious mind —
is now bringing my dreams into physical reality.**

Writing Affirmations

The measure of an affirmation's success is whether or not it
soon manifests in your world. Even if you are affirming something big and expansive, such as a tremendously successful
career, you will start seeing results in your life in a short time,
even if at first it's just a change in your thoughts or feelings, a
change in attitude.

If you continue to affirm without seeing any results, it is only because you are affirming something else on deeper, perhaps less conscious, levels that is creating something contradictory to what you are affirming consciously.

If you're repeating to yourself, for example, *"My connection with infinite intelligence is now bringing me wonderful abundance every day,"* with emotion, and after several weeks you're still broke, then you need to discover what else you have been telling yourself that is creating a contradictory reality. Writing affirmations, and their responses, is a good way to do this.

Get a notebook or a few pieces of paper. (You can do any of this on electronic devices as well — use whatever you're most comfortable with.) On one page, write "Affirmations" across the top. On the next page, write "Thank you!" across the top. Then write your affirmation on the first page. Put your attention into it; pour your feeling into it. You want to be successful, or beautiful, or creative, or whatever — and the truth of the matter is that you deserve it, so you might as well create it for yourself.

Keep writing the same affirmation repeatedly, and keep putting your full attention on it as much as possible. Soon you will probably notice some kind of inner resistance popping up — some words you are telling yourself (affirming to yourself) on deep levels. Whatever they are, write them down on your "Thank you!" page. On this page, voice all of your reactions to your affirmation.

Say you're writing, for example, *"My connection with infinite intelligence..."* and you find yourself thinking, "What connection? That's a total fantasy!" Immediately turn to your "Thank you!" page and write those words. It's called your "Thank you!" page because, as you write those words, you want to mentally thank yourself for sharing them with you (this may sound artificial or strange, perhaps, but it *works*).

Then go back to writing your affirmation *"...is now bringing me wonderful abundance."* Then you may find yourself thinking, "Abundance? Yeah, right! Fat chance!" or "I have no clue how to make serious money!" or even (this was actually said by a close relative of mine), "Rich people are jerks." Write that down, too, on your "Thank you!" page. Then go back and write your affirmation again. And so on.

After writing your affirmation ten or twenty times, you may have ten or twenty or thirty comments on your "Thank you!" page. Look at them carefully — these are the things you are affirming to yourself on a deep, usually unconscious level that are creating your present reality. Sometimes it's enough just to look at them and see how foolish they are, and how they are not really true for you. Sometimes these negative affirmations dissolve as soon as you look at them.

At other times, you may have to create new affirmations that are specifically designed to counteract what you've been telling yourself. In the case above, where you found that you were thinking you could never create a life of abundance, you may want to affirm something like, *"I am capable of creating wonderful abundance in my life, easily and skillfully"* — or, if that's too confronting, lower the gradient for yourself and affirm, *"I am capable of skillfully managing my finances"* or *"I am sensible and in control of my finances; I am creating total financial success, in an easy and relaxed manner, a healthy and positive way."* (That last affirmation did wonders for me; I'm sure it was one of the most powerful things I did that helped me get out of poverty and into a lasting state of abundance.)

Another great affirmation a friend of mine used repeatedly and successfully is: *"I do wonderful work in a wonderful way, with wonderful people for wonderful pay."*

Write your affirmations, note your resistance, then break down that resistance with more affirmations. That's all you need to do. When you finally get to the core of your resistance — to the terrible or hopeless thing about you that you haven't dared to admit even to yourself — when you finally find yourself writing it out on your "Thank you!" page, you'll feel something releasing in you. Then find the affirmation that deals with it directly and releases it for all time.

You'll find yourself feeling wonderful. You are coming into your own power. You are no longer limiting yourself. You're free to be who you want to be, and to create the life you want. It is your birthright.

Save your affirmation pages — they are potent reminders of how powerful you really are. Shred or burn or delete your "Thank you!" pages — they are filled with the negative, limiting thoughts and feelings you are now letting go of and changing into far more positive and expansive thoughts.

Here are some more affirmations. Let them serve as examples for you to create your own:

I am at peace with what is, filled with grace, ease, and lightness.
I have inner peace and contentment — true success!
I have the ability to live the life of my dreams, here and now.
I am living the life of my dreams, here and now.
I am now part of a vast, peaceful army that is transforming the world, in an easy and relaxed manner, a healthy and positive way, in its own perfect time, for the highest good of all.
I am an open channel for endlessly abundant creativity, in many, many forms.
I have wonderful confidence; I am strong and beautiful and serene.
I have beautiful, harmonious, satisfying relationships.
My marriage and family life are filled with grace, love, ease, and lightness.
My times alone are filled with grace, ease, and lightness.
I am in perfect health mentally, physically, emotionally, and spiritually.
Every day, in every way, I am getting better and better.
My income now exceeds my expenses.
My connection with infinite intelligence is now bringing me all the wealth and abundance I wish for.

Spirit flows through me every moment with its healing energy.
I am guided by Spirit, doing God's will.
I am at peace.
Every moment, I feel my Being. This is enlightenment.

Work and play with one, two, or three at a time — as many as you feel you can handle — until you achieve results.

A Common Error

A surprisingly large number of people do something when they begin saying affirmations that prevents them from ever realizing the dream of their affirmations: They assume the affirmations themselves will do all the work and that nothing else needs to be done.

In many cases, it is true that nothing other than saying an affirmation needs to be done. In these cases, all that's necessary is for us to suggest the words to our subconscious, and the forces are set in motion that automatically create what we desire. This is the power of our human energy — our conscious and subconscious states of mind. When you see this happen — as I have many times — it is an exciting and fulfilling experience.

But most affirmations need to be supported by a series of actions in the world. Saying affirmations for abundance or creative expression or the perfect job, for example, needs to be done along with taking logical, concrete steps in the world. These steps are simple to discover; you either know them already, or you can discover them easily by doing a bit of research.

In creating abundance in your life, for example, you have to find the service or product you can offer the world that will shower you with abundance. Then you have to take the steps necessary to make that service or product available: You may need to create a website, make a brochure, make samples, find a way to tell people about your work, and so on.

I have known people who have affirmed abundance and then found an unexpected check in the mail, or an inheritance they hadn't known about. But most people who successfully affirm abundance find that they have to do the necessary groundwork to offer their talents and gifts to the world.

Keep doing your affirmations, and it will become clear to you what you need to do. The steps will become obvious and easy, especially if you keep affirming you are becoming successful *in an easy and relaxed manner, a healthy and positive way, in its own perfect time, for the highest good of all.*

Have Patience

Two more elements are necessary for us to realize our dreams: patience and persistence. Some people are born knowing the value of patience and persistence. Others have to discover it along their winding paths. The world wasn't created in a day.

As many of you have already discovered, sometimes you'll find an affirmation that manifests almost as soon as you say it. But most created things take some time to manifest. Give a seed a week or so to sprout. Then give the plant a few months to grow. Give an affirmation at least three weeks to create some results.

In the case of an affirmation as broad as *"My connection with infinite intelligence is now easily yielding me great abundance in my life,"* it may take years to fully manifest. But you will probably feel some remarkable changes and see some results in your life within a few weeks after affirming it every day. With this affirmation, you'll find yourself having some new ideas about creative ways to make money. You won't be nearly so broke, and you'll be *feeling* a lot more abundant — even if your bank account hasn't changed much in the past few weeks. It will grow, if you are patient and persistent.

One affirmation that worked for me almost instantly was *"I am organized."* For years I had been telling myself that I was disorganized. But as soon as I affirmed to myself, just a few times in a single session, *"I am organized where I need to be,"* I felt something wonderful: I felt the truth of that statement fill my being. I got up from my chair and immediately started listing all the things I was planning to do, hoping to do, and dreaming of doing. Then I organized it all, putting it into a list with the highest priorities at the top.

In one moment, I ceased looking at myself as a limited, unorganized person and instead saw myself as being very capable of clear organization. It was simple. Within a few weeks, I had created a filing system for both personal and business affairs, and I even straightened up my desk and work area somewhat (though, to be honest, my desk continues to be what most people would call a mess, and what I call creative chaos).

If you're ready for it, some of your affirmations may manifest very quickly for you. But it usually takes longer. Just be persistent — keep it up, repeating your affirmations every day (or at least three or four times a week). If a particular affirmation seems to lose energy, if it feels lifeless, if you aren't connecting with it, find another way to say it that feels good and strong to you.

If you see no noticeable results in three weeks, or a month, try writing your affirmations and your resistances. Discover the fear or doubt that is blocking you from creating your good. Then deal with it, one way or another. Let it go. Start affirming words that are the exact opposite of any negative beliefs.

It is startling for most of us when we realize that *we create what we want in our lives.* We may not be creating what we think we want, but in fact we are creating exactly what we want on some deep, perhaps subconscious, level.

If you're broke, it's because you want to be, or because you think it's cool, or because you feel you deserve to be, or because you feel you can't handle money. Whatever the reasons are, you can find some affirmations that will change your thinking. If you're alone, it's because you want to be in the deep parts of your being or because someone told you that you don't deserve love and you believed him or her. If you want to change that, you can. It's up to you. When you want a relationship more than you want to be alone, you'll create it for yourself. All it takes is a strong, focused affirmation with feeling behind it — and patience and persistence.

> **You will be what you will to be....**
> **Be not impatient in delay**
> **but wait as one who understands:**
> **When spirit rises and commands**
> **the gods are ready to obey.**
>
> — Ella Wheeler Wilcox

When your spirit rises and you dare to affirm your greatest good, the creative forces of the universe will rush in to do your will.

The Law of Karma

When working with any of the tools of affirmation, mantra, prayer, or visualization, always keep in mind that it is for the highest good of all concerned. Those who wish to use these tools for what they think is their own good but is at the expense of others or hurts others in any way will create endless problems for themselves.

The law of karma is absolute: The universe is set up so that whatever you do comes back to you. What you sow is what you reap. If you think loving thoughts you live in a loving world. If you think hateful thoughts you live in a hate-filled world. If you hurt someone else, you will be hurt.

This is why there's never any reason to fear misusing these powerful tools, because people who try to harm others, through affirmations or any other means, only end up hurting themselves. The law of karma is infallible.

If you have even the slightest feeling that what you're affirming may not be the best thing for you or for someone else, finish your affirmations with the words, *"This, or something better, is now manifesting for the highest good of all concerned."* Then just sit back and relax and enjoy the fruits of your creation. Let it come to you, easily and effortlessly, without struggling, striving, or suffering.

Easily and Effortlessly

I'll close this chapter by highlighting a particularly powerful affirmation for people in the world today:

"_____ *comes to me, easily and effortlessly.*"

Fill in the blank with whatever you desire.

One of our biggest stumbling blocks in the way of attaining or accomplishing something — especially our most cherished dreams and goals — is that we're trying too hard. The struggle itself becomes a major obstacle.

Life does not have to be a struggle. Look at the trees and plants and animals — are they struggling for survival? As a great teacher said, "Consider the lilies of the field, how they grow; they neither toil nor spin, and yet Solomon in all his glory was not arrayed like one of these."

Simply affirm to yourself,

Love comes to me, easily and effortlessly.
Wonderful abundance comes to me, easily and effortlessly.
Grace and lightness come to me, easily and effortlessly.
Inner peace comes to me, easily and effortlessly.

And you can affirm more specific things, such as,

My perfect artistic expression comes to me, easily and effortlessly.
My book and website project is completed, easily and effortlessly.
Creative success comes to me, easily and effortlessly.
I now have a successful career, easily and effortlessly.
I do wonderful work in a wonderful way, with wonderful friends
    for wonderful pay, easily and effortlessly, for the highest good
    of all.

You can finish even very specific projects and fulfill commitments easily and effortlessly with this affirmation.

When you ask the Universe for something, you will receive it — unless you're denying it on deeper levels of your being. Let it all come to you, easily and effortlessly. You deserve it. You're here to fulfill something wonderful in your life, something you cherish in your heart. And now you are holding in your hands the tools to create whatever your heart desires.

3

Relationships

**We choose our relationships —
whether consciously or unconsciously —
for our growth and evolution.**

Our relationships with others — whether casual or intimate — provide us with a constant, truthful mirror of ourselves. If you have created generally loving, supportive relationships, give yourself some appreciation, for you are obviously being loving and supportive yourself. If you have created difficult relationships, if there's anger and resentment, look into yourself to find the source of those painful emotions.

That other person isn't doing it to you or making you angry; you are doing it to yourself, and you are making yourself angry. In fact, the other person is doing you a big favor by making you aware of your areas of unconsciousness, and pointing out where you need to change in order to create the kind of relationships you want. We should thank those who we have difficult relationships with rather than blaming them: They are our best teachers.

An honest appraisal of our relationships can provide us with some of the best material we have to help us grow. Within the experiences of our relationships are the keys to our freedom. Let's find these keys; they're within us all.

Tantric Relationships

Every relationship we have is a tantric relationship, if we see it in that light. Every relationship is another step on our journey along the path we are creating; our relationships are there to help us learn and grow, every moment. We may not have been conscious of this fact, but there are deep reasons for all our relationships, including those with everyone we happen to encounter, even for a brief moment.

Look at every deep, ongoing relationship you've had. Unless you've been closed off to it, you can see how much you've learned in the moments you've shared. You've each had things to teach the other, and that's one reason you were drawn together. You've mirrored each other in many ways. You've reflected each other's strength and beauty and positive qualities, and you've shown each other where you need to change and grow. And each of you has grown, whether you've wanted to or not.

Sometimes this has been for the good: You've become a clearer, more experienced person in the process. And sometimes it has been a negative process, if the people you've chosen to share your time with have had beliefs (and resulting behavior) that didn't help them or you to become better people. Either way, you change and eventually grow. Either way, it's a tantric relationship, an essential part of your unique path.

What Do You Want?

As we all go along on our various paths, we come to realize that, in our relationships as well as in most other areas of our lives, *we're free to create whatever we desire.* We have evolved enough, as a people and as individuals, to go beyond the need for a single social morality that is dictated to all, and enforced, like the law of Moses. Morality is a purely individual choice, and it is up to each of us to decide in our hearts and minds what is right for us, and to live by that, as long as we don't harm others. We are free to have any kind of relationships we want in our lives.

I learned a startling process from Shakti Gawain (who I think got it from Sondra Ray, author of *I Deserve Love*). Shakti had her workshop participants do it, and it proved to be a real eye-opener for many of them:

Take out a sheet of paper and write three phrases across the top, so they form the heads of three columns:

WHAT I WANT   WHAT I HAVE   WHAT I REALLY WANT

Under "What I want," list what you want in your relationships and in your life in general. Under "What

I have," list what you have at present. Then, under "What I really want," also list *what you have at present* — because we have already created in our lives exactly what we have really wanted.

Some people think this isn't true, because it certainly doesn't seem to be true on our conscious level of awareness. We don't consciously think that we want to be alone, or in unsupportive or unhappy relationships, or in poverty, and so on. But on deeper levels, it is completely true: We have created for ourselves exactly what we have wanted and what we have felt we deserved; we have created what we feel we are worth. But we deserve better things — so let's create them!

First we need to focus within ourselves, and do some inner investigation, and then we'll focus on the outer world of our interactions with others. Almost all the important work, we find, is within. As Eckhart Tolle says so brilliantly in *The Power of Now*,

> **If you get the inside right,**
> **the outside will fall into place.**

Create It Within

We have looked at the forces of creation in our lives; everything begins as a subtle, spiritual impulse, then becomes a thought, then a feeling, and then it is manifested on the outer, material plane.

Whatever we have created so far in our relationships is the result of what we have been affirming to ourselves over the years, the result of what we have been thinking and feeling and believing. Through conscious effort, we can let go of the thoughts and beliefs that are creating what we don't want, and replace them with thoughts and beliefs that create what we do want.

Let go of the belief that you are in any way incapable of satisfying relationships! Quit telling yourself that you don't deserve a good relationship, or that you're selfish or unloving. The truth is you do deserve a wonderful relationship. Underneath it all, you are loving and giving. Refuse to believe that you can't have what you want, because you can, if you *believe* you can.

Let go of all those unsupportive and negative thoughts and beliefs, replace them with some supportive and positive ones, and you will see some very satisfying results, almost instantly. When negative thoughts arise, counter them with positive affirmations and mental imagery. Create an internal picture of yourself as highly capable of having ideal relationships, even if you have to suspend your beliefs to the contrary.

We can't have the relationship we want if we don't have a clear picture or idea of what we want in that relationship. It's essential to get the inside right, get the picture clearly in mind.

Create a clear picture of what you want in a relationship,
and affirm that it is so.
Then see what happens.

Allow yourself to fantasize. Picture your perfect lover. Imagine being together in a beautiful, loving way. Then affirm, *"This, or something better, is now manifesting for the highest good of all concerned."*

If you are involved in a relationship you want to continue, imagine it expanding, getting better and better. Imagine the best possible relationship for all concerned.

A great master once said, "Ask and you shall receive." And yet there are so many who deny this is true, because they have underlying beliefs that life is a struggle and that it's hard to succeed, and so they end up unhappy, unfulfilled. Most of them haven't even asked in the first place. And if you don't ask, you won't receive.

If, instead, we keep asking clearly for what we want — such as a loving, supportive relationship — we will receive it. When we do this inner work, the outer world will reflect it, easily and effortlessly.

The importance of our work on the inner planes in creating anything is in some ways contradictory to what most of us were educated to believe. We habitually deal with things on an outer-directed level, thinking that the thing we need to do in any situation is to go out and *do* something. We think that the thing to do to have the relationship we want is to go meet somebody somewhere — meet that right person. But when we understand that the most important work is the inner work, within our hearts and minds and emotions, we find it much easier to create whatever we desire in our lives.

We simply need to connect, each in our own way, with our abilities to creatively imagine what we wish. You deserve relationships that are loving and supportive. Begin creating them now with a daily affirmation session. Some examples are:

I deserve love!
I feel good about having what I want in relationship.
I am creating a beautiful, harmonious, satisfying relationship.
My relationships are filled with grace, love, ease, and lightness.

Take these words and change them. Make up your own affirmations. And don't ever underestimate or invalidate their power:

Ask and you shall receive.

The Outer World:
Partnership and Communication

As soon as you're ready for a relationship, it happens. Then it becomes something to skillfully manage not only in our inner world but in the outer world as well. All the challenges and problems on the outer plane of our lives are most quickly and easily resolved by going to the inner planes first. Once we get the inside right, our lives become filled with ease and lightness in the things we do in the outer world.

The tantric path is the path of everything. Everything in our lives, and every moment of our lives, becomes our spiritual practice. Every relationship we have is a vital part of our path through the world.

There are two keys to successful relationships — and each one can be summed up in one word. The first is *partnership*. Once we understand this simple concept, our lives become much easier. Every relationship we have is a partnership. We are in partnership with everyone on earth. We're all stuck here in one big dysfunctional family, and families need to get along. The key is to see that we are all partners. We each deserve respect. We deserve to be heard.

Riane Eisler wrote a great book, *The Power of Partnership*, which I highly recommend. Her initial work, *The Chalice and the Blade*, gave us a lens, as she called it, through which to look at history and see two great conflicting forces at work: the power of partnership, symbolized by the chalice, and the power of domination and exploitation, symbolized by the sword. She makes it obvious that the only solutions to our personal and global problems are through the power of partnership. Domination and exploitation will never lead to peace in the world or to peace of mind within.

The other one-word key to wonderful relationships is obvious as soon as we think about it: *communication*. Communication simply means sharing thoughts and feelings — and that includes giving others your honest feedback, both positive and negative, and receiving feedback in a way that's as enlightened as possible.

A fascinating counselor and teacher named Shirley Luthman summed it up this way: There are four possible reactions to feedback, especially if the other person is confronting us in a way that's hard for us to accept.

1. *Denial.* We simply refuse to accept what others are telling us. We tell them that it isn't true, that they don't understand, they're wrong, and so on.

2. *Defense.* We create all kinds of excuses that prevent us from taking responsibility for our actions.

3. *Beating ourselves up.* We admit that others are right, and then create guilt, fear, worry, and a great many other feelings that contribute to a negative self-image.

4. *Simply accepting it and letting it sink in.* This is the only responsible and effective response to have. We simply hear what others are saying, we realize that there is a reason for them to be telling us these particular things at this particular moment, and we accept what they're saying and agree to look at it. If, after a while, we feel their words are valid, we acknowledge that, thank them, and see what we can do to improve the situation. If, on the other hand, after some quiet

introspection, we feel that their communication was not useful for us, we simply let it go, without blaming or judging anyone in the process.

Our friends, lovers, parents, children, bosses, and everyone else we encounter through our day mirror us, giving us valuable lessons that can help us transform the quality of our lives, if we're open to their communications — if we stop denying, defending, and beating ourselves up and instead learn to listen to what they have to say.

Negotiation

Negotiation is an essential skill for communicating in partnership with others. Negotiation can be simply defined as *the art of creating win-win situations*. If either person in the relationship is not winning — that is, not getting what he or she wants and deserves — then the relationship is not working.

So many people plunge into long-term intimate relationships without ever taking the time to sit down together and clearly spell out what each of them wants in the relationship. The result is that they end up spending months or years trying to get what they want while all too often creating frustration and resentment instead.

Most of the time, this frustration can be dissolved with a few simple talks together in which both people communicate as clearly as they can exactly what they want from the other. It's often necessary to compromise, but it is far better to compromise than to spend years trying to get something that your partner doesn't feel good about giving.

Keep focusing on the fact that it is always possible to come up with a creative solution that will give you both what you want. It may be something you've never done before, but there *is* a creative solution. One or both of you may choose to end the relationship — that, too, is a possibility. Separation is usually a better choice than years of frustration. It's up to you, one of the many choices you will make on your winding path through life.

Dealing with Conflict

Conflict will arise; it's an inevitable part of our lives. As Buddha said, "Life is a bitch, and then you die." (This is a great translation of Buddha's *first noble truth* that I saw in big block letters on someone's T-shirt. Fortunately, Buddha had other great truths, including the fact that even though life is a bitch, we don't have to suffer. There is a state of mind that is completely beyond suffering, an inner peace we can all discover.)

There is a simple process that can help us resolve conflicts; we call it "The Argument-Selling Technique." If our politicians and world leaders learned this process, and did it regularly, the world would be a far better place. If you're in conflict with someone, if you're fighting or struggling or stuck in certain positions that don't seem flexible enough to allow you to live or work together, take these six simple steps:

1. Stop. Take a breath. Don't wait for the other person to do it — it takes two to tangle, but it takes only one to stop. The first step in resolving this argument is simply to *stop arguing*.

2. Give your partner time, space, and encouragement to express their feelings. If it has been a heated argument, they might need to rant for a while. Listen to them — don't interrupt them (you'll get your turn). If you do, you're back in the argument. Don't judge them, especially if they're upset. Just let them express themselves, completely. This works wonders to diffuse charges that might have been deeply buried for a long time.

Don't say anything while your partner is speaking. This is very challenging at first, especially if they go on and on and you have several different things you want to respond to. Don't get into negative body language, clearly showing them your reactions in the way you're crossing your arms and sticking out your lower lip and disagreeing. Just stay as relaxed as you can and open to taking in what they're saying.

(The first few times I did this, I even asked if I could take notes while I listened, because I wanted to be sure to respond to everything they were saying. But then I realized there's no need to take any notes because there's no need at all to respond to every point — just the things you remember when it's your turn to respond.)

Sometimes it may seem very difficult not to interrupt to defend yourself or deny or invalidate their point of view. But remember: *Don't interrupt.* Just open up to it and listen to it all. Encourage them to say what is on their mind, even if it's hard for you to take. Wait until your partner has had their say, and then say something like, "Thank you for sharing that with me." I have used this process many times over the years and have found that once someone is able to fully express their feelings without interruption, it never takes more than a few minutes to get to what's really bothering them.

3. *Now respond.* Be sure your partner knows that you want them to give you the time to say what you want to say, just as you have let them do. Tell them they must not interrupt but just listen to what you have to say. They'll get their chance to respond. Then tell them your reactions to what they said; tell them why you're upset, or angry, or hurt, or whatever. Put it out there, even if it sounds stupid or selfish or unflattering. Let yourself say anything that comes to mind about your partner and the situation you've created together. Don't try to edit or censor or soften it — jump into the center of the poison, and show your partner your deepest feelings.

You'll find when you are allowed to speak without interruption you can almost always say what you need to in just a few minutes. Maybe you'll come to realize that even though you think the other person is upsetting you or making you angry, *you're* the one who's upsetting you and making you angry. This insight can instantly resolve a conflict.

The next step depends on how effective the last two have been. You might notice that the charge between you has dissipated, because you've released a lot of the stuff you were holding on to. But if one or both of you still feels agitated, repeat steps 2 and 3. Maybe something your partner just said really made you furious again (even though you *know* that your partner is not making you furious — you're making yourself furious), or sad, or whatever. Express whatever feelings arise. You may have to go around and around steps 2 and 3 several times — and that's fine; at some point you'll begin to feel calmer and closer than you were when you began. Now you're ready for the final steps.

4. Now ask your partner what he or she wants from you. Give them the time and encouragement to tell you exactly what they want and need from you. Listen and remember.

5. Then tell your partner exactly what you want from them. Be open and honest. Spell out what you want and need.

One way to get into it if you have difficulty doing this is to play a little game together in which you ask yourself what your *ideal scene* is in this situation. If you could be, have, and do things exactly as you would want, what would it look like? This leads us right into the final step:

6. Negotiation. Don't shy away from this word because it sounds too cold or businesslike. (Or if you just don't like the word for some reason, pick something else that works for you, such as *making agreements*.) Negotiation is a basic part of every relationship: We are together because we have some reason for being together, and that reason involves giving something and receiving something from the other person. If the relationship isn't working smoothly, it is because the agreements haven't been spelled out clearly enough.

Now that you've each discovered what your partner wants from you, you can make some clear agreements. When you do this once the argument has dissipated, in a spirit of closeness and respect, your negotiation can turn in all kinds of creative directions. There are limitless possibilities! Ask for what you want, and find some area of agreement with your partner. You may have to compromise, but never allow one person to disrespect or in any way violate the other. Somehow, both of you can find agreements you both feel good about.

If this practice doesn't work for you, if going through these steps doesn't clear the air and resolve your feelings, you may need to seek a counselor or skilled facilitator or mediator to help the two of you share your feelings in an effective way.

Our deepest tantric relationships bring out our deepest feelings and emotional patterns, and a lot of us need help learning to explore and express our feelings in a way that doesn't create more negativity. All too often we tend to "dump" negative feelings on our partners, criticizing them or blaming them rather than staying with our own deepest feelings and expressing them in a way that is honest, even vulnerable, and that doesn't deny the other's feelings.

Enlightened relationships are just like enlightened business: They are a win-win proposition. Everybody wins, nobody loses. You've heard what your partner wants from you, and you tell them what you feel good about giving them. Tell them what things you can do for them and what things you cannot do.

You'll find yourself getting really creative in the negotiation stage. There are no set norms or forms that you have to follow. A great change is taking place in the mass consciousness, a change that allows all people to live their lives as they wish. Every one of us is free to have any type of relationship we want — so what do you want?

Every relationship has the potential to become a perfect relationship. There are all kinds of things we can do to make this happen in the outer world, but of course the simplest, quickest, and most direct way to create the perfect relationship is to do it within, in your mind and heart.

**Get the inside right
and the outside will fall into place.**

Keep remembering both the inner and outer levels of activity in your relationships. You always have the option to go within yourself, and get the inside right, and you always have the opportunity to open up to others and work out a win-win relationship.

Some people find the inner plane easier to deal with, and some find they are more skillful on the outer. The key is to learn to deal with them both, balancing them in your unique way.

Jealousy, Fear, and Anger

Jealousy is all too common for many people. It is a deep, subtle, sometimes even violent conglomeration of emotions — mostly fear and anger. Like all emotions, it is something to be respected, and something to be examined.

The most important step in creating any kind of true, deep freedom within a relationship is to totally accept the feelings of jealousy you, and your lover (or lovers), may have. It's okay to be you, it's okay for them to be themselves, it's okay to be jealous, and angry, and fearful.

Accept your feelings, completely. This is the first step toward rising above them and transmuting them into the highest creative energies. When we fully accept our feelings — yes, there is a patch of poison growing right across our path — we no longer give those feelings the power of our resistance. What we resist stays with us. Once we let go of our resistance, we can truly let everything go that we don't want to hold on to. This is a key to freedom and enlightenment.

We must first accept jealousy, anger, and fear; then, as we teach ourselves how to let them go, they will soon dissolve. This can become our focus: to accept the jealousy, fear, and anger in ourselves and in others completely, and then to find the means to let them go.

Our focus becomes a matter of finding *skillful means* — means that are different in each different situation, and for each different person. Skillful means are endless, just as the path of our evolution is endless.

Keep this in mind in all your relationships with others: You can create whatever kinds of relationships your heart desires. You can have completely loving relationships with as many or as few people as you want. Monogamy is wonderful for most people; for some people, it isn't. It's up to you.

Remember, too, that it is your small self, your limited self, that is behind any separation you feel from anyone. And it is your higher self that is moving into openness, love, and oneness with others.

Don't reject your feelings of separation and jealousy and anger and fear. Just accept them, and let them pass. You don't need them at all. Affirm to yourself something like this:

I am open, to all people at all times…
Like the sun, I shine my light on everyone…
I am an open vessel, filled with divine love…

A Key to Fulfilling Relationships

Give your lovers — and everyone else in your life — the freedom to be themselves, and find the freedom in your heart to be yourself. Trust and support the other person's power, and trust and support your own. They are not in conflict. There is always a way to harmonize your feelings with your lover's feelings.

Trust and support the other person's experiences, insights, impulses, dreams. Support each other, and encourage each other to do what feels best in your hearts. It may mean spending time alone, or being apart at times. Let it be.

Give your sharing a huge space in which to move, and grow, a space large enough for both of you, all of you, to be completely fulfilled.

There are an infinite number of approaches to solving any problem that comes up in relationship. Be creative — trust your own experience, your own feelings, for these give you the answers you are looking for, the ways to work it out.

You choose your relationships, consciously or unconsciously. They are happening, and they are happening for a very good reason, whether you know it or not. They are happening as part of your evolution, part of your growth into true freedom and creativity and happiness.

Love is the answer
Love is the key
It can open any door
Give us eyes to see
In our hearts lies a secret
And it set us free:
All we need is love...
All we need is love!

4

Sex

**It is time we saw sex as
the truly sacred act it is:
It unites us with the forces of creation,
showing us the wonder of what is.
It is a path to enlightenment.**

I would like to extend a warm welcome to all of you who are beginning to read this book at this chapter. I'd probably do the same thing. Sex is a vital force, a force to be understood, and dealt with — and yet so many people have not dealt with it effectively! They run from it, or feel trapped in it or frustrated with it, or keep searching for it — and find no satisfaction in any of these choices.

The great teaching of tantra is that we can find inner peace and joy by plunging into every feeling, every desire, every moment — rejecting nothing, as long as we don't hurt anyone.

Any activity whatsoever, if gone into deeply enough,
will lead to ultimate understanding, freedom,
and peace.

This includes our sex lives.

Some Questions for You to Answer

Take an honest look at your attitudes toward sex. Do you like
it? Do you want it? Do parts of it seem shameful or immoral?
Should you have it with only one person? Are you basically
monogamous? Polygamous? Asexual? Are you satisfied with
your present sexual situation? Could it be improved? Do you
have any views or feelings about sex that might be holding you
back from living the kind of life you would love to live?

It doesn't matter how you answer these questions. You are a free
being — your true nature is already absolutely free. So you can
feel any way you want about sex, or relationships, or marriage, or
anything and everything else. But if you find that your views and
beliefs are limiting your freedom, or hurting you in some way, or
keeping you from getting what you want in life, it's very useful to
take a good, clear look at those beliefs. Plunge into them, examine them, and describe them clearly to yourself.

Whatever your sex life currently is, you might as well feel good
about it! You're creating it for yourself, so you must have good
reasons. You may or may not be conscious of this, of course.

But you can become conscious of it right now — if you just think about it for a moment.

The first step is to be totally honest. How have you felt about your sexual relationships? Do you have regrets about anything? Do you feel guilty about anything? Take some time to examine that one — guilt is a popular state of mind in our culture.

Trust Yourself!

The world has changed. The idea that we have a right to life, liberty, and the pursuit of happiness has caught on. We're free to be ourselves. We've learned that you can't dictate or legislate morality: Everyone has their own inner moral sense and is free to act accordingly — as long as they don't violate anyone else's rights to life, liberty, and the pursuit of happiness.

The best guidance is always found within you. Trust and respect your own impulses, your own feelings. Trust that your inner guidance will lead you to discover the life and lifestyle perfect for you. If you follow your feelings, you'll never go wrong. You may do something extreme — if so, you'll find a much greater clarity about yourself afterward, if you examine your feelings carefully and honestly.

It's all right to do something extreme once in a while. I have a rule of thumb about this: *Everything in moderation — and that includes some excess (in moderation).*

I've known so many people who are excessively moderate, and underneath all their moderation is a fear of their deepest feelings and impulses — they're afraid of themselves, and stuck in rigid models of what they should and should not do. This kind of moderation will never help us become truly free.

Sexual Energy

A beautiful, dynamic source of energy in the universe is waiting to be tapped — the energy of creation.

We've all experienced this energy. When you put a man and a woman together, you have the energy of creation. (Or, if you prefer, you can say that when you put two women or two men together, you have the energy of creation — tantra embraces everything, rejecting nothing, so of course it embraces gay lifestyles and every other lifestyle as well. Don't be put off by the male-female language in this book. Substitute your own changes wherever necessary.)

Much has been written and taught about *transmuting* sexual energy. For most of us, however, this is unnecessary and redundant, for sexual energy transmutes itself. When our sexual energy moves through our bodies, we experience a physical, mental, and emotional transmutation of that energy. This happens whether we're making love, meditating, or masturbating.

How does this take place? Our body is an energy system, and different parts of our bodies are different centers of energy. Our sexual center contains a very powerful source of energy, and when we focus on it by physically arousing it or mentally concentrating on it, we find that it is a *dynamic* force — it moves.

When we let it move as it will, we find that its natural movement is upward, through our abdomen, into our hearts, and still further upward into higher centers of energy and glandular activity in the throat, the forehead, and the crown of the head. This energy can then literally shower over our entire being, rejuvenating, purifying, healing, strengthening. Making love opens our hearts and expands our minds. It raises our consciousness, and connects us with the infinite so powerfully that even atheists find themselves shouting, "Oh, God!"

Many people, trying to be either moral or spiritual, cut themselves off from their sources of power in their so-called lower centers of energy. Many people on spiritual paths believe, as those in Shakespeare's time did, that an orgasm is a "little death," something that dissipates life energy. And some teachers from India teach that sexual orgasm weakens the system, and that the energy needs to be held in and drawn up into the higher centers to awaken true freedom and enlightenment. The result — except for those rare few who just aren't suited for sexual expression — is repression, self-denial, and guilt.

I know, because I've tried that path. And I've known many others who have tried it — and many who are still trying. I found that celibacy doesn't work for most of us, at least in the West. It requires too much denial of our feelings, desires, and impulses. It leads to a rejection of ourselves and our culture, and even, in a very basic way, a rejection of the life force itself.

I don't mean to deny the value of celibacy for those who feel they're getting something worthwhile out of it. Tantra embraces all paths — even the path of those who deny or withhold their sexual energy. The path of tantra teaches us to accept everyone and every other path, even those who criticize or condemn us for saying what we have to say.

Every person must find their own path,
in their own heart.

For most of us, sexual energy is something to be celebrated, enjoyed, and used as a great vehicle to propel us forward on our path to liberation and light. This is the path of tantra.

Our bodies are miraculous creations. They're to be respected, admired, appreciated, enjoyed. A deep truth that emerges from spiritual study is that we are all God-like beings; we have created our phenomenal bodies through our own DNA; we have grown ourselves from infancy to maturity. If we believe God is omnipresent, that means God is in every cell of our bodies. So when one person admires another walking down the street, it is God admiring God's own creation. And the one being admired is also God enjoying God's own creation.

Sex is more than a natural impulse — it is a deeply sacred act. When two bodies are joined, a very special temple is created through the force of two spirits, two energy fields, blending into one. A powerful energy flows between the two bodies that is deeply healing, strengthening, refreshing. It is a profound opening…a letting go…a perfect, wordless meditation on the creative forces of life.

Tantric Sex

Ancient tantric sex practices are described, sometimes literally, sometimes symbolically, in many books. Two amazing tantric temples still stand in India, adorned with thousands of statues in different sexual positions and practices (although, from what I have heard, the Indian guides to these temples seem embarrassed by them, and tell people that they are somehow metaphorical rather than physical, when the statues are obviously explicit and extremely un-Victorian).

Many of the ancient tantric practices involve elaborate preparations that celebrate all the senses — including different foods and wine for taste, flowers for sight, incense for smell, bells and other musical instruments for sound, and our bodies for touch. The most important element in the sexual practices is the acceptance and enjoyment of all the things that give us pleasure, and an appreciation of beauty.

Some teachers define tantric sex as sex in which you don't reach an orgasm but meditate deeply together for a long period. This is a beautiful way to make love — but certainly not the only way to make love. In my opinion, tantric sex includes all kinds of sex, rejecting nothing. Come if you wish, or don't come — whatever your heart desires.

There is nothing to reject in our sexual energy and our sexual relationships — there is beauty in each moment of our lives.

There is nothing to reject;
there is beauty and wonder
in each eternal moment here and now.

Create your own tantric practices — and they'll be the best practices of all for you. You are free to do whatever you wish. You're free to live out your deepest, most soaring fantasies.

One Beautiful Way to Make Love

Here's one specific practice. Let it serve as a model for you to create your own. Adapt it in any way you wish.

Lie with your partner, or sit together. Bask in the beautiful simplicity of just being with each other, silently.

See, and enjoy, and caress each other's bodies....

At some time, the man says to the woman, focusing on her body, "This is the temple." At some time, the woman says to the man, focusing on his body, "This is the temple."

At some time, the woman focuses on the man's sexual center of energy and says, "This is the key to the temple." At some time, the man focuses on the woman's sexual center and says, "This is the entrance to the temple."

Then the key is slowly and gently placed into the entrance...and each says, in their own way, in their own time, in their own words, "We are in the temple, receiving the blessings of the Universe."

(Words here are optional, because you may want to just go on without words.)

Now feel, as completely and as sensitively as you can, the creative energy of the Universe flowing through you, blessing you, giving you eternal youth, eternal vitality.

Feel how good it is to be alive...you are life itself....
Feel your oneness with all of existence....
Feel your natural divinity....

The energy within flows from your sexual area to the highest levels of consciousness....

You are one with All....

You are light, you are life.

It is time we saw sex as the truly sacred act it is: It unites us with the forces of creation, showing us the wonder of what is. It is a true path to enlightenment.

Sustaining Sexual Energy

Some men — especially young men — can find it difficult to sustain their sexual energy long enough to give their partners a truly deep and fulfilling experience. Stimulation is so intense for men that they can find it difficult to control. A few simple techniques can help give the man as much control when making love as he wishes, allowing him to reach a climax just as his partner does.

The first technique is mental; the others are physical:

1. In your mind's eye, circulate the energy through your body when making love. The intense stimulation is centered purely in your sexual center, so move the energy up your spine and circulate it around your body and your partner's body. This allows you to make love for much longer.

2. When deeply united with your partner, if the man moves more in a circular pattern than in a straight in-and-out pattern, the lovemaking will last much longer. This is more exciting for the woman, generally, and a bit less exciting for the man, giving the woman more time to catch up with the man's level of excitement.

3. The final technique is part of the "chaotic meditation" that was taught by Bhagwan Rajneesh, a well-known teacher and prolific author from India. If you do this exercise, you will probably discover that it strengthens you sexually, giving you the control to prolong and enjoy sex as long as you want.

Do it when you're alone. It may seem peculiar — but give it a try. I don't, however, recommend it to anyone with a heart condition, because it is very strenuous.

Put your hands up over your head, and jump up and down vigorously for ten minutes while shouting, "Hu!" with force every time you land on your feet. Breathe from your diaphragm — deeply, down in your stomach, and lower.

After two minutes, you'll probably be exhausted. But go beyond your imaginary physical limits, and you'll find that you can jump for ten minutes quite easily, once you get into it. Don't strain, but do jump energetically.

Then relax.

Afterward, you'll find that the muscles in your abdominal area are much stronger, and that you have a source of power and energy within you that is much more potent than anything you might have imagined. Strenuous sit-ups would probably have the same effect.

Making Love

One golden sunlit morning, my partner and I began to make love in our large bed, with windows on two sides and sunlight streaming in through the trees. I felt the energy rise through my body as we got more deeply involved; soon it seemed to be connecting us with the sunlight, connecting us with the source of creation. It was ecstatic.

At that moment, I heard a voice, almost shouting — euphorically — in my mind...and I realized it was a strange sort of poem. I tried to ignore it but couldn't — it demanded to be written down. So I had to excuse myself for a moment, find a pen and paper, and scribble down the first verse. Then we went back to our lovemaking. Then I heard a second verse, and a third. I have no idea how long it took, but when we were through, the poem was finished.

It says a great deal about the deep truths of tantra. The word *dakinis* in the third line is a word from India and Tibet referring to angels or, more accurately, females of both the physical and spirit world who have attained great wisdom and power and are teachers of many people in ancient Eastern tantric traditions.

Making Love

I remember every lover
    With such sweet feelings
I dream of divine *dakinis*
    With such sweet prayer
Every woman is a blessing —
    God's creation
Every body is a miracle —
    The mind's revelation

Every moment of love —
    Sweet inspiration!
Every one is Divine
    As they open to their depths
Such exquisite ritual
    Sweet meditation!
The forces of creation
    Unfolding within us
The Kingdom of Heaven
    Is truly within us

Remember the myths
From our deep past heritage —
Leda and the Swan…
Europa and the Bull…
The form of God appearing
In a shower of gold
To a woman of exquisite
Divine earthly beauty!

In love are all the teachings —
The deep truths of tantra —
In love are all the forces
Of the Universe on display
For all to see, to catch,
To understand
And to enjoy the Bliss
Of Union of the Divine

Within every woman —
The forces of the Moon
Within every man —
The forces of the Sun
Moon unites with the Sun
Eclipsing into One
And a New Moon is born,
And we are reborn,
Continually reborn!

Within every woman —
    The forces of the Earth
Within every man —
    The forces of the Skies
Earth and Sky unite
    And Heaven is here!
Totally illumined,
    If we but understand it
Totally blissed
    With vision Divine

If the Universe provides
    You with a lover,
Make love! Enjoy!
    Unite with the Divine
And if the Universe shows you
    You're to be alone,
Reflect! Enjoy!
    Unite with the Divine

    for —

The greatest blessing
    Of all in love is that
It's always ever
    Within us

We're man and woman
Old and young
The union is ever
Within us

So we don't have to hold on
To anyone else
We don't need a lover
To be in love
God takes care
Of all His creations
Even alone,
We're never alone
Mother Nature takes care
Of all Her creations
Even alone,
We're always all one

A Meditation for Lovemaking

Do you want to meet the perfect lover? Or become the perfect lover? Try a meditation similar to this:

Sit, or lie down, so that you're very comfortable.

Take a breath, exhale, and relax your body, from head to toe....

Take another deep breath, exhale, and relax your mind, let all thought go....

Take another breath, exhale, and let everything go....

Do this a few more times, if you wish, until you're completely relaxed.

Now picture yourself meeting your perfect lover. Picture the two of you touching. Picture yourself possessing all the qualities you desire in a perfect lover. Picture yourself making love, easily, effortlessly, and beautifully.

Affirm something like this (find the affirmations that feel just right for you):

My ideal lover has come to me, easily and effortlessly.
I am open and spontaneous — a perfectly satisfying lover!
I am now the perfect lover, with my perfect lover.
Every day, in every way, I am getting better and better.

Take a moment or two to enjoy your fantasy. If you do this kind of visualization — and if you don't afterward cancel it out with negative thoughts or visualizations — it will soon manifest for you, in an easy and relaxed manner, a healthy and positive way, in its own perfect time, for the highest good of all.

A Life-Changing Practice

One night in my dreams, a song was sung to me. One of the lines is something I have often reflected on and often repeated:

**There is nothing to reject;
there is beauty and wonder
in each eternal moment, here and now.**

Turn this into a practice, and it will change your life.

Practice seeing the beauty in everyone…and the beauty and wonder in yourself. All creation is a miracle, if you look at it that way. Every friend, every lover, everyone you meet, everyone you see, has their own unique beauty…their own unique face of God, or spark of the divine, that they reflect. Can you see it?

Every lover you've ever had and will ever have is a divine being, in their essence, in their true being. Can you see it?

Their bodies are miraculous creations of a loving divine force, and by loving them you have united with that force….

And the most beautiful part of it all is that the same is true for them, because when you see the divine in them, they see the divine in you.

5

Being Alone

**To be alone is to tune into
the sacred being of yourself.**

Being alone and enjoying it is a fine art that has almost become a lost art in the world today. A recent poll found that being alone is one of the major fears of people throughout the world. That's a sad fact, because being alone is one of our greatest opportunities for growth and creativity.

Look at the great visionaries throughout history. Their visions, their deep insights and true understanding, always came to them in their times of aloneness. To be alone is to realize the sacred being you are.

If you enjoy being alone, you are well on your way to discovering the joys and wonders that every moment of your life can bring you. If you don't enjoy being alone, there are several things you can do to change it. You're going to be alone some of the time anyway, so you might as well learn to enjoy it.

Self-Examination

One of the most powerful techniques for overcoming the fear of being alone is simply self-examination. Look directly — without avoiding *anything* — at all the things you fear about being alone, all the things that make you uncomfortable. Look at what is going through your mind when you are alone. Do it gently, with respect, and without judgment or guilt. Clearly see all the things you tell yourself. Pay attention to the thoughts, and the songs, and anything else that goes through your mind.

Watch your thoughts and feelings. That's all you need to do. Watch them arise, observe them when they dominate your consciousness, and let them go. Notice that these thoughts and feelings do pass — all things pass. And they pass much more quickly if you are able to observe them, clearly and openly, without rejecting them.

The Self-Questioning Process

If you are still having difficulty being alone, it can be very helpful to go through the self-questioning process described in chapter 1 (under the head "A Tantric Practice"):

Ask yourself, "What am I feeling?" or "What am I telling myself?" Tell yourself the first answer that pops into your head, and then say, "Thank you!" to yourself. Then ask it again, and again, if necessary, as many times as you need to until you get an answer that feels good to you, or until something feels resolved within you in some way.

If you keep going, you get deeper and deeper answers to your questions, and then you find the question and answer that dissolve your difficulties. There's no need to fear being alone. You are an infinitely creative being — and it is usually much easier to tap into your full creative potential when you're alone than when you're with others.

A Meditation on Being Alone

When you're alone, you are open to receiving the guidance of your intuitive mind. A meditation like this one can help you find your connection to the wise, wonderful, powerful teacher and guide you have within you.

Sit comfortably. Take a breath and relax your body as you exhale....

Take another breath and, as you exhale, relax your mind and let all thought go....

Take another deep, slow breath and, as you exhale, let everything go....

Sit and tune into your presence within....

Bask in the radiant light energy that fills your body, mind, and spirit....

Feel the wonder of your being, something always with you, now and forever....

Pick some affirmations to repeat that feel particularly good to you in the moment. Some suggestions:

I love being alone.
I love the blessed inner wonder of my solitude.
In my aloneness, deep understanding is revealed to me.
Every day, in every way, my life is getting better and better.
I am in touch with my intuitive mind; it is clear and ever present.
I am open to receiving everything I need to know, and everything I need to have.
I am enough.
I have everything I need to enjoy my here and now.
In our darkest moments, our brightest treasures can be found.
To be alone is to know my sacred being.
I am now connecting with the wise, wonderful, powerful teacher I have within....
I am bathing in the light of my conscious awareness within....

Enjoy your time alone. There are deep teachings to be found within these special moments — if you give yourself time to hear your inner intuitive teacher.

Listen Your Way to Enlightenment

There are a vast number of excellent audio programs that are worth listening to when you're alone, when you want something uplifting and inspiring, or deeply relaxing.

Find the words that connect with you most deeply, and listen repeatedly. Repeating powerful words enough times to drill them deeply into your memory and subconscious mind is one of the fastest, most direct ways to propel you forward on your path to fulfilling your dreams.

In the beginning was the Word.

You Don't Need a Lover to Be in Love

When we're young, if we're blessed, we have had the wonderful experience of falling in love. We gaze on someone beautiful, and our whole world becomes beautiful — sweet, miraculous, filled with light, and with the wonder of life itself.

We think it's the other person who causes it all, and when he or she leaves we are bereft, and our hearts are broken.

At some point we realize, if we're blessed, that our love comes from within us, not from that other person.

And we realize we don't need to depend on anyone else; we don't need a lover to be in love.

We just need to see the wonder of what is.

We just need to love, love, love.

That's all.

6

Work

By focusing on your short-range needs,
you can lose your long-range sight....
Focus on your highest purpose in life,
your deepest wishes, your most precious dreams.

Buckminster Fuller once said that he realized as a young man that it was no longer necessary to work for a living, since we have reached a level of automation and productivity that no longer requires that everyone has to labor for their sustenance. He spent several years looking at what needed to be done for humankind, and for the planet in general. He followed his intuition and his dreams, and proceeded not only to have a spectacular career but also to make a number of important contributions to humanity and to the world.

Look at Your Beliefs

Look at your beliefs about work. Are they limiting you in any way? So many people have never asked themselves that question — and it's a question that can transform their lives!

As we know by now, our beliefs form the inner foundation that creates our outer experience of the world. If we believe we have to work for at least forty hours a week doing something we dislike or that we consider menial or uncreative, we find that the world fully supports our belief, and it seems impossible to do anything but work to provide ourselves with the bare necessities of life.

But there are alternatives, especially when we realize that this is just one kind of belief (a limiting and all-too-popular one), and that many other people with different belief systems have been highly successful in achieving their goals and dreams, and creating exactly the kind of life they want for themselves.

If you have a set of beliefs that are not serving your highest purpose in life, you can examine them and realize they can be changed. Even your deepest, longest-held beliefs can be replaced with newer ones that serve you (and humanity, and the world) far better. Affirmations are powerful tools for changing even our deepest core beliefs. If you're not satisfied with your present life situation, look at your belief structure, and find the affirmations that will help you change it.

When you get down to it, the single most powerfully motivating force that keeps many people in jobs they dislike is *fear* — fear of not having enough, fear of not making it without working at that job. Affirm your fears away. Remember that when you are following your intuitive guidance and acting for your highest good, the universe will always take care of you — you will always have enough.

I left a very secure full-time job to start a very insecure publishing business that proceeded to lose a great deal of money in its first three years. Leaving that regularly paying job was not easy — it took a leap into the unknown. (My leap was assisted, I must confess, when I was fired from my secure job for not showing up on time. That turned out to be a blessing in disguise!)

I knew on some level that I was compromising myself, limiting my full potential, by continuing in that job. And I knew the universe would support me — though I didn't know exactly how. And it has, of course, as it always does. Using simple, repetitive affirmations, I slowly weeded out my beliefs of struggle and limitation — *It's so hard to succeed, you have to struggle to survive* — and ended up creating far more abundance and wealth in my life than I could even dream of. I live very comfortably, with a lifestyle that allows me to work for myself when and only when I feel like working. It's a dream come true.

You can do the same — if you wish — if you affirm things like this:

Every day, in every way, I am getting better and better.
My success comes to me, easily and effortlessly.
In an easy and relaxed manner, a healthy and positive way,

in its own perfect time, for the highest good of all, I am
now creating ... (finish the sentence as you wish).
I do wonderful work in a wonderful way, with wonderful
people for wonderful pay.

Your Highest Purpose

So many people work just to survive. And this takes so much time and energy that they neglect their deepest desires and dreams and creative talents. By focusing primarily on your short-term needs — food, rent or mortgage payments, clothes, dental and medical bills, and so on — you can lose your long-range vision.

Be sure to take some time to focus instead on your highest purpose in life, your deepest wishes, your most expansive dreams. Then find or create work that is in alignment with these things, and you will find that the details of your life will fall into place as you become more and more aligned with your highest purpose. This process can take some time to unfold, but it is a journey well worth making.

Your Ideal Scene

Some people have difficulty discovering their highest purpose. It has been so long since they have taken the time and energy to focus on their greater purposes that they've forgotten what they are. Take the time to play this little game: It's powerful enough to create profound, lasting changes in your life. I did this the day I turned thirty, and it is not an exaggeration to say that it dramatically changed my life.

Take a sheet of paper, and write *Ideal Scene* at the top. Imagine you are suddenly five years in the future, and during the five years that have passed, you have been completely inspired, and you have brilliantly managed to create everything your heart desires. Allow yourself to be completely fanciful and unrealistic. You have succeeded beyond your wildest dreams.

What does your life look like? Describe where you live, what you do, how much money you make, what kind of relationships you have, and so on. Usually a single page is enough for you to get a broad, clear picture of what you want in life.

Play with this, just as children play at being what they want to be when they grow up. If you could have anything you want, what would it be?

Have fun with this practice. Allow your fantasies to wander, and explore all kinds of different possibilities, if you feel like it. This isn't just child's play — it could have a very concrete effect on your future. You now have the perspective to sketch out both long-term and short-term goals and dreams for yourself.

Take another sheet of paper and write *Goals and Dreams* at the top. Then list every goal you can think of, both long- and short-term.

Every general goal can be broken down into several specific goals. Every specific goal can be broken down into the specific steps necessary to accomplish that goal. Take the next obvious steps in front of you; you'll find they are always small, doable steps. Keep focusing on your goals, keep affirming they are manifesting, and you will soon find yourself living in a world you only dreamed about a short time before.

Don't ever fear being trapped by your goals — you can always change or delete them, if and when you feel like it.

Now that you have explored your ideal scene, now that you have taken your dreams out of the closet and listed your goals, you are in the right state of mind to write — in a short, simple paragraph — your highest purpose in life.

Take another sheet of paper and write *My Highest Purpose* at the top. Then start writing a paragraph beginning with "My highest purpose is..." and complete the sentence. Use no more than one short paragraph to express it.

Even though they're written in broad, general terms, these words that come from your heart and soul can be like a lighthouse that guides you on your journey toward the destination of your dreams.

Once you have your ideal scene, your highest purpose, and your goals clearly listed in front of you, you are in a much better position to determine exactly what you want to do with your valuable time and energy than you were before. This is the key to finding what has been called *right livelihood* — work that is aligned with your highest purpose as well as with your dreams and goals.

This is the only kind of work that will be deeply satisfying for you. When you're fulfilling your purpose in some way, you are working with a powerful energy that helps you to accomplish even more than you ever dared to dream of originally. It may require a leap of faith, a leap into the unknown — but you will never regret making it.

A Meditation to Create the Perfect Work for You

As with everything else, it is essential to create a clear picture of success on inner planes before it can manifest on outer planes in the so-called real world. Try the following meditation, and see what happens:

Take a few minutes to relax.

If you just have a few minutes, simply take a deep breath and, as you exhale, affirm to yourself, *"My body is now relaxing."*

Take another deep breath, and affirm to yourself as you exhale, *"My mind is now relaxing."*

Take a third deep breath, and as you exhale, let everything go...

Now, if you have ten minutes or more, you can do the longer version. If you want to do the shorter version, just skip this next part and move right on to the affirmations at the end:

Take a deep breath and, as you exhale, relax your feet. Take another deep breath and, as you exhale, relax your ankles.

Continue a deep, rhythmic breathing, and as you exhale, move up through your entire body, letting each part go: calves, knees, thighs, butt (first chakra), sexual area (second chakra), lower back, stomach, diaphragm (third chakra), midback, heart, lungs (fourth chakra), upper back, shoulders, neck (fifth chakra), back of head, face (sixth chakra), top of head (seventh chakra)...

Now you're relaxed, deeply. Enjoy the feeling of your deep relaxation....

Feel your presence within....

Imagine yourself, in your mind's eye, doing exactly the kind of work you most want to do. Try to see it as clearly as you can — though if you can't see clearly, that's okay; just imagine it, creatively, in any way you can.

Play with it, like a child. Have fun with it.
Imagine how you spend your time.
Imagine your work environment.
Imagine getting paid for your work.
Imagine yourself being totally satisfied and happy with your work and its rewards.

Affirm something like:

I do wonderful work in a wonderful way, with wonderful people for wonderful pay.
The Universe provides, abundantly.
My perfect, creative work comes to me, easily and effortlessly.
My connection with infinite intelligence shows me my perfect work and play in the world.
I am now creative and fulfilled.
I am now creating my ideal success, in an easy and relaxed manner, a healthy and positive way, in its own perfect time, for the highest good of all.

I can accomplish anything my heart desires.

Make up any others that feel good to you.
Then, take a deep breath, and affirm,

**This, or something better, is now manifesting
in totally satisfying and harmonious ways,
for the highest good of all.**

Take one more deep breath and, in your own time and
in your own way, return to your waking consciousness,
feeling relaxed and refreshed.

You don't have to have a clear visual image of your goals and
dreams, and you don't have to see how to get from where you
are at present to where you dream of going. If you just consistently imagine the final situation, the vast power of your subconscious will show you how to get there.

If you do the meditation to create your perfect work every day
for even a short while, you will definitely see some results in
your life, and they might be startling. You will have a much
more effective work attitude and work situation. Soon you'll
find clear, insightful, creative ideas drifting through your mind,
in an easy and relaxed manner, that will transform your work
into something that is totally, wonderfully aligned with your
highest purpose in the world.

Be persistent, and don't worry about how you will achieve your lofty dreams. The means will become clear to you — as long as you keep your dreams in mind, especially the end results of those dreams.

Enjoy Your Work!

It's good to see, too, that whatever you are doing now has its own perfect reason for being and its own perfect teaching for you, and it can be satisfying in its own way. Very monotonous, routine work, for example, is excellent practice for mindfulness — watching your thoughts, being in the moment.

And many people find great satisfaction and fulfillment in doing work that in itself is mundane but that serves others in their family or community. Enjoy your work — regardless of what you are doing, and regardless of whether you desire to be doing something else. You'll discover all kinds of new rewards when you're able to do this. And you'll discover the direct, effective path of tantra — using every moment as an opportunity to grow, seeing every moment as a vital step on your spiritual path.

> **This is the path of tantra:**
> **Seeing every moment as a stepping-stone**
> **to a higher state of evolution.**

A Prayer

Creator of all that is,
I thank you for my work,
I thank you for my life.

I thank you for showing me how to do what I love,
and make it my work in the world,
work that abundantly supports me and so many others.

I thank you for the life energy that courses through me,
the gift of life I have been given,
precious beyond words.

7

Money

**We are as limited,
or as unlimited,
as we imagine ourselves to be.**

Now we're getting down to the bottom line.

It's certainly appealing to a lot of us to realize that the path of making money in life can be a spiritual path as well, if we look at it that way. Along the way, as we learn more and more about making money, we learn about right livelihood. We learn about the power of the Golden Rule, and see that it is a great key to wonderful, lasting success: *Do unto others as you would have them do unto you.*

Here's an excellent, brief process Shakti Gawain and I did at some of our workshops. It just takes a few minutes — and the rest of the chapter will be far more meaningful for you if you actually make this little list:

Take a piece of paper, and at the top, write "Money is..." and then underneath, list everything — good, bad, irrelevant, weird, embarrassing, whatever — that comes to mind about money.

List the things you've heard about money. List the things you tell yourself about money. Just take five or ten minutes, and you'll probably get all the big ones down...or take a little longer if you feel like you're avoiding something.

If you're like most people, the list — whatever you wrote — probably has a lot of contradictory feelings and ideas on it. Now reflect on this thought for a moment: *Money is none of those things*...money itself is nothing at all, except what we make it.

Money is really a very mystical thing. It's just paper, with some ink on it, some letters and numbers and designs on it — very similar to this page you are reading, if you're reading this as a print book. In itself money has no value at all but is simply a medium of exchange, a convention set up to assist people in trading one thing for another in an efficient way. And yet we have so many conflicting attitudes and feelings about it.

Look over your list again — look at how you feel and what you think about money. It is good, it is bad; it's something we need, and something that corrupts. Can you see how these beliefs have created your experience of your financial situation? Can you see that your beliefs about money are self-fulfilling, like all beliefs? Can you see that you can have it any way you want it — if you change your beliefs?

We can have as much or as little money as we want. In fact, we *do* have as much or as little money as we want. This is explained by what I call my *cool theory*: Everyone affirms and therefore creates exactly the lifestyle they think is cool — or right, or appropriate for them. The way you're presently living your life is the way you think is best, or you think you deserve, on your deepest levels of being. If you want to make changes in your life, you've got to change those deep inner beliefs, through your creative meditation and affirmation, through the power of your own imagination. It can be done, and the results can be spectacular.

You don't need to struggle for money, or feel pressured by money. It's only necessary to understand the principles by which it operates (and they're really quite simple), and to make your own choices about how much you want to create for yourself.

Throughout my twenties and early thirties, I obviously thought it was cool to have very little money. In my thirties, however, I decided to change all that. It was a simple, conscious decision: I had changed, and I now thought it was cool to have abundance in my life, and that included having a good deal of money. I started affirming these words — and I really do believe that, after probably a few thousand repetitions over several months, these words had a powerful impact on my life, because I managed to completely overcome my deeply held beliefs that I was a fool with money, and out of control:

I am sensible and in control of my finances.
I am creating total financial success,
in an easy and relaxed manner,
a healthy and positive way,
in its own perfect time,
for the highest good of all.

I have created a life of abundance, based on the belief that the universe supports me, comfortably, wherever I go, whatever I do. This change in my life was relatively easy for me to create, simply by examining my underlying beliefs about money, and about my lifestyle in general, and by changing those beliefs through creative meditation and that one powerful affirmation.

It's quite amazing to see how quickly your entire world can change as a result of a small amount of effective inner work. Get the inside right, and the outside will fall into place, easily and effortlessly.

Let Go of Limiting Beliefs

We create our experience of the world out of our deepest underlying beliefs about ourselves and our world. This is a deep, powerful teaching, once you grasp it — one that gets to the essence of the path of tantra. Most people think it works the other way around: The world is a certain way, and so we develop our "realistic" beliefs as a result of what the world imposes on us. The world is beyond my control; I am a victim of fate and circumstances.

But I encourage and challenge you to try this other view on for size, and see what happens. What if it is true that our deepest beliefs create our experience of the world? If so, shouldn't we take the time to examine these beliefs and become familiar with them? If we use the process of self-questioning we saw in chapter 1, it's easy to do.

It's not all that difficult to discover where these beliefs come from — they usually come from parents, peer groups, media, or people we respect or admire. Some of these beliefs are useful and supportive; many are limiting and unnecessary. And they can be changed — have no doubt about that.

You are in complete control of your life. Certainly no one else is! You create your own experience constantly, based on your underlying beliefs of who you are, what you deserve, and what the world is like, reflected constantly in your mind through what you are telling yourself as a result of those beliefs.

Look at what you are telling yourself. Become aware of the stream of words going through your mind. So many people are simply not aware of their thought processes. Focus on your thoughts, and observe them objectively. Let the negative, limiting ones go. Focus instead on others that serve you better and that are closer to the reality you wish to create for yourself.

Any thoughts of lack or limitation are unnecessary. You can do anything you like. You can create any kind of lifestyle you want. You can have as much money as you like — it's true, if you believe it to be true. As Henry Ford famously said, *"If you think you can, or if you think you can't, you're right."*

Another very wise person, Richard Bach, put it this way in his book *Illusions*: *"Argue for your limitations, and they are yours."* That's it, in a nutshell. We are as limited or as unlimited as we imagine ourselves to be.

Let go of your limiting beliefs.
Imagine your greatness instead,
and it is yours.

This is not an overstatement. You can be great. It's up to you, for you are the original powerful creator of your life and your world. You are not a helpless victim, overwhelmed by forces beyond your control, unless you believe you are. You can change that belief to something far better for you: You are a brilliant, creative person who is finding the perfect way to live the life of your dreams, in an easy and relaxed manner, a healthy and positive way, in its own perfect time, for the highest good of all.

A Creative Meditation for Money

Try the following meditation, and watch it produce some tangible results — often in a very short time:

Get comfortable, close your eyes....

Relax, in any way you wish....

Feel your presence, your creative life energy within....

That warm, vibrating energy within you is in everything around you, too....

You are completely connected to the life energy of the whole universe.

Now just imagine, in any way you can, that the abundant energy of the universe is coming to you, filling you with lightness and fullness.

Imagine that energy takes the form of money in some way.

You can simply feel it as an energy that you are attracting.

Or you can see it as green bills, or as checks in the mail, or as gold.

Imagine it coming from one direction, then another, then another.

Imagine it coming from every direction.

Feel the abundance of the universe showering you with money.

Affirm, with energy, words such as:
I am open to receiving the blessings of an abundant universe.
Money comes to me, easily and effortlessly.
My income exceeds my expenses, always.
I am a source of abundance in an abundant universe.
My connection with infinite intelligence is now yielding me a fortune.

As you are saying these affirmations, imagine your mind connected with a focal point of energy in the universe that is showering you with abundance and wealth.

Try this meditation daily for a week or so, and watch for some very pleasant things to come your way. I did this quite often for a while, and still do it occasionally, lying flat on my back, along with a visualization of perfect health, and of effortlessly accomplishing whatever projects there are to be done.

When you do this kind of meditation, you are conditioning your powerful and vast subconscious to receive even greater good in many different forms. Your subconscious will respond, in its own way, by giving you ideas, suggestions, "hunches." Follow up on these ideas, even if they seem impulsive. Many will be very fruitful. And if they aren't, nothing has been lost, and a great deal of experience has been gained.

Creating Abundance

Sometimes we use the word *abundance* when we're thinking specifically of money; when we affirm for abundance in our lives, we're really thinking about a good improvement in our cash flow and bank account. It can be very liberating, personally and financially, to see that creating money and creating abundance are at their core two very different things — and that abundance is relatively easy to create.

Many people who have a substantial amount of money still have not created a feeling of abundance for themselves, and they are often worried about expenses, rising costs, taxes, investments, and the future. And there are people with very little money who have a feeling of abundance, and who live in a world where there is always more than enough of everything. For *abundance is a state of mind* — a state of mind that you can consciously create, with the power of your mind.

We live in an abundant universe: Look at the number of stars in the sky — there are at least 100 billion known galaxies, with an average of 200 or 300 billion or more suns each. Look at the number of seeds on an oak or eucalyptus tree, or a dandelion. We are surrounded by infinite abundance, if we stop cutting ourselves off from it, open up to it, and let ourselves be part of it.

Start seeing yourself, right now, as living in a state of abundance. The size of your bank account doesn't matter in the least. The only thing that matters is your state of mind, which is always clearly reflected to you by the things you are telling yourself. Start telling yourself that you are an abundant being, in an abundant universe, filled with gratitude for the vast wonder of what is.

So be it. So it is.

The 10 Percent Plan

Years ago I developed a system of money management that has helped me in my winding path from poverty and limitation to abundance. So many people, regardless of their level of income, tend to spend whatever they make. When I first started making some money and then had regular and dramatic salary increases, I still kept spending whatever I earned — even more than I earned, getting into credit card debt.

Then I decided to start saving 10 percent of my income — in effect, tithing to myself. I realized that if I always had enough with whatever amount of money I was making, I would always have enough just spending 90 percent of what I made. At first my savings didn't seem to amount to much — but after about six months, it suddenly felt like a sizeable amount, and I started investing it in the stock market to get a better rate of return.

Of course, 10 percent is purely arbitrary. Over the years I have met people who saved 20 percent, even 50 percent or more. Once I started saving 10 percent, I went through a time when I'd raid my savings for large purchases I just had to make. The solution to this, for me at least, was to set up another account I called the Large Purchases account, and I put 10 percent into that account as well as into savings.

Do whatever works for you, but set up a simple framework in which you save, invest, and make large purchases and still have money to cover your other expenses. You can do it; it's not that complicated.

We live in an abundant universe.

If we have the underlying belief that life is abundant, we don't have to worry about inflation, or recessions, or depressions. We will always create enough for ourselves and our families. And in so doing, we are able to assist others around us in overcoming their negative conditioning through our positive example.

Some people made fortunes during the Great Depression. They refused to believe what the newspapers were saying and what everyone else was believing, and they used their creative imaginations to see that there are opportunities everywhere to tap into the abundance of the universe, an abundance available to any and all of us.

To Sum It Up

The great truths can be expressed simply. This truth bears repeating and remembering:

Ask and you shall receive.

Ask for the money, the lifestyle, the things you dream of and want in your heart. Ask for it in any way that feels good to you. Ask for it in prayer. Ask for it in meditation — visualize it coming to you. *Ask, and you will receive* — that is the law of the universe, reflecting the power of creative thoughts and words. Just try it and you'll see the powerful truth of these words.

8

Creativity

You are a creative being.
Know it. Accept it. Enjoy it.
There are infinite possibilities...
and you're dreaming of them every day.

Our culture has been very progressive and successful in some ways — and an abysmal failure in others. One of the greatest failures of our educational system involves creativity. Every child is a creative genius. Children draw, sing, dance, make up stories and songs, conjure imaginary friends, play fanciful games, and do all kinds of other creative things with abandon. They are directly connected with their intuition, the source of all creativity.

Then we send these children to school. In all too many cases, their natural intuitive spontaneity is ignored and even denied, and they are forced to sit at a desk for six hours a day while they are drilled constantly into believing that education is the accumulation of a huge number of rational facts. Schools teach children that they are stupid if they don't know all these facts.

Their natural creative genius is not reinforced, and all too often it withers away. The result is a society in which most adults feel they're not very creative.

I'm sure my experience is typical in some ways. I was considered a bright, successful student. But I secretly felt that I didn't know anything. I felt the only thing I learned in school was how to impress teachers rather than how to truly learn and grow. I have a feeling that most students, whether successful or not, essentially learn — on a deep, perhaps subconscious level — that they don't know much of anything, that they are basically stupid and uncreative. At least, that was my experience.

Getting a higher education was, for me, even worse. I was primarily interested in theater and English — two highly creative fields. Perhaps my experience would have been different if I had been a business administration major, or a physical education major. I hope so. Because the things I learned at the university caused me to shut down rather than open up my creative potential even more.

In English classes, we analyzed other people's writings so much that very few of us felt we could write anything ourselves. Poetry seemed so complex — because of the teachers' detailed, rational analysis of every phrase — that I felt I would never be capable of writing any good poetry. It was far too dense and difficult.

Outwardly, I appeared to be a success in school — I graduated Phi Beta Kappa amid all kinds of obsolete ceremonies and speeches. But inwardly, I was dry, shut down, and cynical — this was the result of my higher education!

It wasn't until six years after I left the university that I was able to write anything. And unfortunately there are many others in creative fields who've had a similar experience. After a while, though, I finally forgot the teachers and the analysis and gradually became able to write again. It took me several years, but I was able to connect with my innate creativity again.

I'm not saying there are no good schools and universities. I'm simply relating my experience. Many people have had a very different experience in school, fortunately. But whether your experience was good or bad doesn't really matter in the long run: You can become as creative as you want to be. You can let your spirit soar.

Unlocking Your Creative Genius

Every person is a creative genius. Perhaps you can't accept that statement — perhaps you feel, like so many others, that the word *genius* should be reserved for a chosen few, like Einstein and Bach and Michelangelo and any others you feel have gone far beyond the accomplishments of most people. But I use *genius* in a broader sense: A genius is one who is connected with his or her intuitive nature.

We all have an intuitive sense, and we're using it all the time. We simply need to become more aware of what we're naturally doing all the time, and in doing so we unlock the genius within us. Our creativity opens up, easily and effortlessly, and poetry, books, music, crafts, skills, and all kinds of other satisfying creative things spring from us, spontaneously.

There are many different ways to unlock the creative genius within you. One is by remembering and reconnecting with the fantasies, dreams, and activities you had as a child. What did you dream of doing and being? What did you actually do when you were much younger? Remember it, connect with it, and *act* on it. Get out your old crayons, or sit down and write something, or start making something — whatever you have an impulse to do. You'll never regret it.

Another way to open up your innate creativity is to tune into your deepest dreams and fantasies that have continued to surface for you all your life. What creative things do you imagine yourself doing?

Simply imagining something takes you several vitally important steps toward its completion. And it's the most important part of any project — the visionary part. Without the initial vision, nothing is accomplished.

> **Don't underestimate the power of your fantasies**
> **and daydreams.**
> **Within them lies the power to create**
> **whatever your heart desires.**

Perhaps the most powerful method of all for opening up your creativity is meditation and affirmation. We'll get to that in a moment — but first, let's deal with the obstacles to unlocking the creative forces within you.

Dealing with the Inner Critic

What is blocking your natural flow of creativity? For most people, the greatest obstacles to creativity — and to a life of joy and freedom in general — are internal and external critics and judges and the negative self-images that those criticisms and judgments have produced.

Throughout our formative childhood and our school years, many people criticized and judged our capabilities and activities. Unconsciously, we gave these critics and judges the power to affect us. As a result, we felt inadequate and guilty in many ways — and our creative channels dried up.

Let go of all judgments of yourself, both those that come from within you and those that other people give you. Don't give these judgments the power to affect you. Understand that they are not serving your greatest good — unless, of course, those judgments happen to be positive and supportive.

Whenever you find that you are critically judging yourself, simply let go of that thought and replace it with something more supportive, such as, *"I am talented and highly creative"* or *"I am connected with my intuitive intelligence."*

Whenever you find your Inner Critic disparaging your dreams in any way, say clearly and firmly something like, "Look, Inner Critic. You are a very valuable part of me; you have discriminating wisdom, and can show me how to go about accomplishing my dreams. But I refuse to let you shoot my dreams down. I want your support, not your criticism. I insist on it, in fact."

I've known writers and other artists who have visualized locking up their Inner Critics while they do their first round of creative work. Whether you are dancing, writing, painting, starting a business, building a career — or *whatever* — give yourself encouragement to launch into it without criticizing or judging yourself, especially at first, when your ideas are most vulnerable to criticism and judgments.

It's easy to see this in the process in writing. You can't write a book and critically edit it at the same time. If you try, you block yourself, usually on the first sentence. You have to find a way to tune into your inner creative voice and get that critic out of the way, at least at first. You have to write initially without judging or editing in any way. Once you have finished your first rough pages, then you can invite that Inner Critic back in to help you edit those pages and make them better. Your Inner Critic is an excellent editor — but a lousy writer.

I have a friend who is a highly successful writer and teacher. He once told me that one of his fondest childhood memories was of his mother tucking him into bed at night. Every night she told him, "There's nothing you can't do in your life — you can do anything and be anything you want!" With early conditioning like that, no wonder he was successful. Whenever we find that we're being hard on ourselves, we should give ourselves some positive encouragement instead, telling ourselves just what my friend's mother said to him.

Fear of Failure

Another great — and unnecessary — obstacle to our full creative expression and to our fulfillment and success in life is the fear of failure. This, too, can be let go of — there is no need at all to fear failure.

The Course in Miracles has it exactly right: There are only two basic human emotions, love and fear, and all the others spring from them. When we dare to dream, we naturally focus on what we love, and love becomes the driving force that helps us realize our greatest dreams. Henry David Thoreau put it simply and clearly:

> **There must be the generating force of love
> behind every effort destined to be successful.**

When our fears arise, they can be powerful enough to overshadow our natural, innate love. If we give more attention to our doubts and fears than to the things we love, our efforts will not be successful. It's that simple: Focus on your fears, and you will create the things you fear. Focus on what you love, and you will create what you love. What we focus on most consistently in our minds soon becomes our reality in the world.

Fear of failure prevents so many people from realizing their dreams. And yet fear of failure can be overcome — and once it is, there are no limits to the life you can create for yourself. There is no need to fear failure. All our fears are unfounded, ultimately, and failure is no exception.

There really is no such thing as failure anyway, because every "failure" is just another lesson to be learned on the way to your success — if you see it that way, if you look at it through the lens of love rather than fear. The trial-and-error process is our natural process of growth — look how many times children learning to walk fall down, but they get right up and very soon they're walking and running with great energy and skill. If we feared every fall we're destined to take, we'd still be sitting in our cribs.

Look at the truly great people of history. Almost all of them experienced many so-called failures before achieving success. They simply didn't give others the power to judge them, and they didn't fear failure.

Give yourself as much support and encouragement as you give to a child you love who is doing something new and fresh — like taking a first step. You deserve just as much praise and support in your first creative steps of any kind of project — no matter how small those steps may seem.

A Ten-Minute Practice

Take ten minutes (or, if that's too intimidating, take five, or two) to give yourself a bit of time to open up your creativity. Just decide that you'll spend the next ten minutes doing something new and creative, something you've fantasized about, something you've dreamed of doing, perhaps, but somehow have never gotten around to doing.

Take a few deep breaths, and relax....

Now just decide to do something creative during the next few minutes, and do whatever pops into your mind.

Give yourself total freedom to do anything. Write a poem or something...dance...make up a song...sing something...play something...make something...invent something...start a creative project of some kind ...imagine something...change something around....

Do it now!

One woman who came to a workshop I gave said she had been intending *for years* to write poetry but never got around to it because she kept telling herself that she had to have everything organized in her house before she could write. She had been promising herself that she would start writing as soon as she finished cleaning her home and organizing her closets, and somehow she never got around to finishing her tasks.

Many of us are doing similar things with our creative energy — finding all kinds of absurd ways to postpone expressing ourselves. The woman in the workshop simply looked at what she was doing, decided it was totally unnecessary to wait until her closets were organized before writing something, and made a commitment to herself that she would write her first poem within two days. It worked. Now she's written a whole book of poetry.

What if Shakespeare or Emily Dickinson had waited until their closets were clean? We'd be missing some great writing.

A Tantric Musician

I once lived in a little cottage on the grounds of an old mansion. There were several other little cottages around, tucked in the woods. In one lived an older man who rarely came outside — I saw him only once or twice in several months and thought he was a hermit of some kind. A friend of mine saw him one day, sitting in the afternoon sun near his cottage. She got to talking with him and asked him what he did. He said he was a musician, and he invited her in to hear him play.

He seemed friendly, and so she agreed and went into his place. It was dark and cluttered. One entire wall was covered with stacks of newspapers, piled over six feet high. A bunch of sticks had been jammed into the newspapers, and hanging on the sticks were various objects — pie tins, pot covers, cups, all sorts of things that make a sound when struck. He picked up two spoons and started playing the objects on the wall. Then he handed her some spoons, and they played together. She loved it! She had never played anything before, but suddenly she was an instant musician and got right into it.

Why not? There have been nights when several of us have gotten into playing our kitchen — banging on pots and pans and the stove and refrigerator and everything else around.

When you're free, you're free to do whatever you feel like doing. Don't judge yourself for it. Just get into it, and enjoy it. The creative possibilities are endless.

A Meditation for Opening Up Creativity

Give the following creative meditation a try. Make up your own variations to assist you with your own particular forms of creative expression.

Sit or lie comfortably. Close your eyes, take a deep breath, and relax....

Feel all stress and tension release, from the top of your head down through your body and out your feet....

Feel the radiant light energy that fills your body....

Imagine that your body is an empty vessel, an open channel for the creative energy of the universe.

Imagine creative energy flowing through you, healing you, relaxing you, uplifting you, inspiring you....

Now imagine yourself doing some specific thing you dream of doing. For example, see the book you've wanted to write being completed, easily and effort-lessly. Imagine how it looks when it's printed and bound. Imagine holding it in your hands and admiring it, feeling pleased and grateful.

Take a fantasy journey, and see yourself as a master of whatever art or craft or business enterprise you wish. See yourself doing the things you want to do. See peo-ple appreciating you and supporting you abundantly in your creative expression.

Affirm to yourself words such as:
I am an open channel of creativity.
*I am a vessel for endlessly abundant creativity, in many,
    many forms.*
Creativity comes to me, naturally and spontaneously.
I am connected with my intuitive mind.
*My intuitive awareness is easily surfacing, opening up all
    my creative channels.*
*_____ (the name of your creative project)
    is completed, easily and effortlessly.*
I am connected to the master within me.

Make up your own affirmations.

Then take a deep breath, and come out of your meditative relaxation, feeling light and refreshed. Take a moment to enjoy your creation, and to appreciate your unique, wonderful creative energy.

All creation begins from within. Have fun with this meditation. Start right now to enjoy your own unique creativity.

Some Great Advice

When I was a teenager I was in a play written and directed by a creative genius named John Donahue. He gave me some dialogue that I was having some trouble with. I don't remember now what the problem was exactly or what question I asked him, but I have never forgotten his response to it: He just looked at me and said, *"Cut the shit and do the thing."* And then he walked away.

He was like a Zen master who gives his students koans to meditate on, and I have often reflected on those words and have applied them to all kinds of different situations. They have helped me cut through a great deal of garbage and lame excuses that over the years had blocked my natural creative expression.

You, too, are a creative being. Know it. Accept it. Enjoy it. Cut the excuses and do the thing. There are infinite possibilities... and you're dreaming of them every day.

9

Food and Drink

When people make their thoughts pure,
all their food is pure.

— James Allen, *As You Think*

There is a long poem from the Chinese tradition of Buddhism called *Shodoka*, written in the eighth century CE. One verse of it goes like this:

Release your hold on earth, water, fire, wind
Drink and eat as you wish in the Nirvana mind
All things are transient and completely empty —
This is the great Enlightenment of the Buddha.

Natural foods are now part of mainstream culture, and that's been good for our health. Rates of heart disease are decreasing, for example, as more and more people are exercising and eating a healthier diet, with less meat and refined sugar.

But our interest in natural foods has been a mixed blessing, for with it has come an awareness that results in a lot of negative conditioning for some people, and downright fanaticism for others. Too many people vehemently affirm to themselves and their children that sugar, white flour, salt, meat, coffee, alcohol — and even in some cases eggs and dairy products — are harmful, even poisonous substances, dangerous to their health.

Those beliefs end up creating a massive amount of guilt every time these folks have an ice cream cone. They're telling their children that white sugar makes them manic and sick. These words — like any other affirmations, positive and negative — tend to become self-fulfilling prophecies if they're repeated often enough.

**It is far more important what you tell yourself
than what you actually eat and drink.**

It is far more important what you think and say about your eating habits than what you actually eat. It is certainly true that some foods are better for your body than others. My stomach usually feels more content after a bowl of yogurt than after a meal of canned corned beef hash. My body clearly tells me what it wants and doesn't want. So does yours. Trust your body, and listen to what's going through your head, especially whenever it's telling you that what you're eating is bad for you.

In my early twenties I was a vegetarian for several years. While the diet was definitely good for my body, I became so rigid it was hard to relate to the rest of humanity. I couldn't stand the sight or smell of meat and felt that people who ate it were obviously on a far lower level of consciousness than I was. I was a health-food chauvinist.

Then I met and studied with a Tibetan lama, a teacher who glowed with radiant health, and who loved meat, especially greasy, fried meat (loaded with garlic and ginger, I have to add, and their benefits definitely help to overcome the unhealthy impact of all the fat). He never ate his vegetables, and he laughed at people's food fetishes. He taught me many things, including the importance of eating and enjoying whatever you want, without being neurotic about it.

I eat and drink whatever I want. I like to wait until I'm good and hungry and then eat exactly what my body wants. Whatever I eat and drink, I affirm that it's all good for my body. These are powerful words to repeat to your subconscious mind: *I am in perfect health, physically, mentally, emotionally, and spiritually.*

A Tantric Experiment

There was a time in my midtwenties when I got passionately into white sugar. Every afternoon, I'd go to my favorite doughnut shop and have a huge, gloppy, sugary mess that I looked forward to intensely and enjoyed immensely. But I'd leave with a lot of mixed feelings along with my sugar buzz, so I knew something was going on.

I decided to do something about it, and thought of several possibilities, from going cold turkey to overindulgence. I decided to try a tantric experiment. I went to the doughnut shop and ordered *four* huge, gloppy, sweet things, and a cup of coffee. I ate every one of the doughnuts, and ordered three more, and another cup of coffee.

The woman behind the counter looked at me as if I was totally crazy. And, in a way, she was right — but there was a method to my madness. I launched into the second batch when suddenly my body started screaming, *"Stop! Enough! Yuck! This is crazy!"* So I left, feeling somewhat nauseous and buzzy from all that sugar and coffee.

The next day I felt absolutely no desire for sweets of any kind. In fact, I've been quite moderate with my sugar intake ever since. I can take it or leave it; I'm no longer craving it.

You Are Not What You Eat

By taking our eating so seriously, and by telling ourselves "you are what you eat," not only are we denying ourselves a lot of enjoyment, but we're also denying our body's incredible strength and its natural healing and cleansing abilities. We are much more than what we eat. We are physical beings with bodies that heal themselves; we're emotional beings with feelings that guide us intuitively; we are mental beings with the power to create our bodies and our life experience through our mind's creative energies; and we are spiritual beings, one with all, united on the deepest levels of our being with the whole Universe. We are much more than what we eat.

I'm not suggesting that you use the tantric perspective as an excuse to abuse your body in any way. If you're not healthy, your body is giving you messages, telling you what you need to eat and drink and do in order to be healthy again. Love your body, trust your body, and give it what it wants. And it will serve you well.

A Meditation

Relax, close your eyes, take some deep breaths....

As you exhale, relax even more deeply, and affirm, "*It feels so good to deeply relax.*"

Turn within, and feel your body filled with glowing, healing light....

See and feel your body in perfect, radiant health....

Feel the life energy pouring through you, cleansing and healing you.

Affirm something like:

My body is in perfect health.

My body is perfectly pure and healthy.

I always tune into my body and eat exactly what's best for me.

Whatever I eat is good for me.

I am in perfect health, physically, mentally, emotionally, and spiritually.

So be it — so it is!

10

Meditation and Yoga

Transformation is here and now —
it happens in the present moment,
not in the past or future.

Meditation and yoga are excellent for us, physically, emotionally, mentally, and spiritually — but, like everything else, they, too, can turn into addictions and other neurotic behavior that end up blocking us, preventing us from the real wonders and benefits of these ancient techniques and traditions.

Don't ever put yourself down because you can't meditate or you aren't meditating enough or you missed your yoga session or can't hold your downward dog long enough. That's using a good tool for a bad effect.

The Benefits

Physically, your body can be healed and strengthened through meditation and yoga. Regular physical yoga practices help us avoid a great number of expensive medical bills. Meditation of any kind brings a heightened awareness to your body, so you become very sensitive to its tensions, its energy, its state of health. That in itself can heal a great many physical problems, and prevent a great many others.

Simple, silent meditation in itself purifies and heals your body over a period of time. I first heard this said by a Zen master named Katsuki Sekida (1893–1987), author of the great books *Zen Training, Two Zen Classics*, and *A Guide to Zen*. He predicted that in the future there would be many studies about the physical, mental, and emotional benefits of meditation. He was right.

Emotionally, meditation and yoga have beneficial effects that are immediately obvious. They calm emotion, without repressing. You usually feel good after meditating or doing yoga. Even if you're in a state of emotional turmoil, a grounding in meditation and yoga can give you a healthy distance from your emotions, so your whole experience becomes less intense, less important and serious.

You realize emotions come and go, changing all the time. And you realize you are *not* your emotions — you are a far greater field of awareness that your emotions and thoughts arise in and pass through. You realize — you come to feel and know in every cell of your body — that you have an awareness that is far greater than your emotions, and that awareness is calm, clear, peaceful, and deep. That's what you can find in meditation and yoga. They can bring a lasting inner peace that is always present, regardless of outside circumstances.

Meditation can help tune you into your feelings in a way that is clarifying and ultimately even enlightening: Through meditation you can grow to understand the true nature of your emotions and of yourself. Your emotions are an essential part of your experience, something to be embraced, and something from which you can learn a great deal about yourself. For within our emotions are the doors to our intuitive understanding — the source of our knowledge, power, and enlightenment.

Mentally, meditation and yoga have wonderful effects as well. They can clarify and simplify difficult problems or decisions. They calm a rampant, active mind: If you are going on and on about something excessively, without a satisfying resolution, a simple quiet period of meditation can give you some distance from your thought processes and allow you to see it from a much clearer perspective. Often a simple solution will appear without any effort at all.

We've all experienced the healing and clarifying effects of a good night's sleep. When a problem seems intractable, we say we'll "sleep on it," and in the morning the resolution has appeared, easily and effortlessly, in our minds. The same thing can happen with a period of meditation, even a short one.

Meditation helps you to stop identifying so completely with your thoughts, your feelings, and your body. You come to realize that you are something beyond all these things — for these things are changing all the time. There is a deeper, more constant thread that runs through your entire being. Whatever words we pick to describe it lack something; we can call it your spiritual nature, or your divine essence, or simply your being.

Spiritually, meditation and yoga have the greatest effect, for they can give you the deep knowledge of who you really are: You are, in reality, one with everything, part of a single quantum field, an integral part of the Universe.

On the spiritual level of understanding — the highest plane of knowledge — there is no distinction between things, for all things, at their core, are of the same substance, which is pure energy. You are one with a blade of grass, a tree, a star.

**You are the life energy
of the Universe.**

You are endlessly being nourished by this energy...you are eternally being reborn.

The Pitfalls

The pitfalls of meditation and yoga can be summed up in a very useful rule of thumb that can be applied to any and all psychological or spiritual theories and practices:

If it dissolves neuroses, it is good for you.
If it creates more neuroses than it dissolves,
let it go.

The most brilliant teachings in the world, like our greatest scientific discoveries, can be either skillfully used or unskillfully misused. It's up to you to discover whether the practices you are doing are solving problems or creating them. Don't be afraid to move on to new experiences if your heart is telling you that you can grow more by trying something else.

Meditation

Meditation takes endless forms, from the totally passive meditation of silence — in which you simply sit or lie down, and let all thoughts go, until you are eventually in a state of complete, wordless, wonderful silence — to highly active forms such as the visualization and affirmations and guided meditations that are given throughout this book.

Take some time to do some meditation…some silent practices …some stress-reducing relaxation…some magic…some creative visualization…whatever you want to call it, whatever you want to do.

Do it slowly…in an easy and relaxed manner…and make your connections, each in your own way, with your inner truth… your infinite intelligence.

If we take the time, now, to do this well, we will make a connection in this moment that is forever with us, at our call, effortlessly, because it is a part of our being — it is our spiritual nature. It is what is.

Transformation is here and now.
It happens in the present moment, not in the past or future.

Silence

Take a moment to just sit in silence....Something will happen, deep in you, even if it seems like nothing is happening at all....Something wonderful can emerge from a moment of silence, something you could never experience through words. Take two minutes, or half an hour, or an hour — whatever you want.

Just sit or lie very comfortably....

Take some time to relax your body and mind by consciously letting go of any tension you discover as you relax, from the crown of your head to the soles of your feet and into the earth....

Now sit in silence. As thoughts arise, simply let them go.

Just sit in silence.

You might have experiences in this silent meditation, or you might not. It might seem like nothing happens at all. It might even take months or years, but at some point you will suddenly realize something of great and lasting value that you gained from those moments of sitting in silence.

There are many different approaches to finding the silence within:

A Zen approach:
Sit there and do nothing and find your own way....

A Tibetan approach:
Find the silence between your thoughts, and stay in that silence for a while....Look into the space between your thoughts...what is the space between your thoughts?

A traditional Buddhist approach:
When you experience a thought, say to yourself, "That was a thought," and let it go....Don't judge it, don't reject it, don't dwell on it, just let it go and return to silence.

At first it might seem as if you're inundated, overwhelmed with a vast number of thoughts rushing in. But keep at it, and you'll soon be rewarded with something wonderful: an experience of silence.

Or it might be an experience of fulfillment, in some deep way, or of a discovery that changes your life. You might even experience the complete perfection of yourself, and of every moment of your life.

It's certainly worth trying; it might turn out to be a lot more rewarding than watching old reruns on TV.

The Active Forms of Meditation

Now we'll turn to some of the more active forms of meditation, those involving visualization. Don't worry if you can't visualize clearly. It doesn't matter at all. Simply imagine it, feel it, in any way you can, and focus your attention on it.

**Even if your inner vision is so shimmering,
so light that it is hardly there at all,
it has great power.**

The vaguest shimmerings can live on in your memory with as much meaning and impact as the clearest inner visions. We can remember the things we imagine in our mind's inner eye as clearly as all the other outer activities of our active lives.

In the deepest sense, you are visualizing all the time, in your mind, in your imagination. It's a magical power we were all born with. These active forms of meditation contain the essence of true magic, for they can, with repeated use, focus our creative minds in a way that deeply influences the power of our subconscious. And once our subconscious mind has been given the instructions to create something, it can and will do it — for our subconscious connects us with the forces of creation, and then gives us operating instructions, blueprints for the creation of what we dream and desire.

We are all creative beings. And we can have whatever we truly want, if we but understand these principles and apply them repeatedly for a while. Try some of the following active meditations, and see how they feel. If nothing else, do the "Creative Meditation," and see if it has some surprising results.

The first meditations prepare you to expand, help you to heal, and increase your goodness and power in the world.

Pillar of Light

Here's a brief meditation — five or ten minutes long, or longer if you wish — that has powerful healing effects on mind and body. It helps us let go of all imagined limitations and imagine the life of our dreams.

Sit comfortably...relax....

Close your eyes, take several deep breaths, and relax more deeply....

Relax from the top of your head to the bottom of your feet....

Let all tension flow out of you, down into the earth....

Enjoy the feeling...it feels so good to relax deeply....

Feel your presence within....

A shimmering field of light and energy....

Now imagine that your spine is a beautiful, shimmering energy field....

Energy flows up and down your spine, and it is light and healing....

It dissolves all tensions....

The pillar has an opening at the bottom — at the base of your spine, going down to the soles of your feet....

This opening sends that energy deeply into the earth....

And the earth sends energy up through that opening, from its greatest depths — right from the center of the earth....

Feel that energy moving through you, grounding you....

Once you are grounded, you are free to soar to any heights you wish, and there is never anything to fear or reject....

The pillar opens up at the top as well....

It opens into the universe....

It is our connection with the cosmos....

There is a high, shimmering, electric energy that we can feel, and that we can, at will, run through our spines, top to bottom to top....

Tune into it, gently....

It is a warm, shimmering light energy at the top of your skull....

It is your crown chakra, your connection with infinite intelligence....

We are a microcosm — one with the macrocosm.

We are children of earth and children of light.

Feel the healing energy that flows through your body....

As you breathe in, feel the energy of the earth rise up the open pillar of your spine....

Feel it rise right up through the top, uniting with the energy of the universe....

As you breathe out, feel it shower over the top of you, a golden, etheric Fountain of Life....

Feel it flow down through you, and into the earth once again, cleansing, filling you with light, dissolving all obstacles....

Repeat the breath, several times, imagining, as you breathe in, a vital, healing, glowing, subtle spiritual energy rising up the beautiful tube of your spine, all the way up through the top of your head....

Imagine, as you breathe out, this energy showering down over your whole body, in a fountain of light....

And, as you breathe in, the light collects beneath you and rises through you again....

And, as you breathe out, the light showers over you again, in a pyramid of golden, healing light.

This light is a blessing for you, from your highest self.

Relax...enjoy it...bask in it....

It clarifies and heals your whole being....

You can send it within you to heal anything and everything, to be in perfect health.

And you can send this light energy to anyone you wish, anyone who needs a healing or a blessing from you through the power of your imagination.

Simply raise your hands, palms out, and visualize sending someone the healing energy that is flowing through you....

See her bathed in it....

Feel him healed by it....

See them in perfect health....

Take a deep breath as you finish your meditation, and enjoy the peace and pleasure of your relaxed body....

Open your eyes, gaze around you, and know that every moment, waking or sleeping, you are bathed in the energy of the creative forces of the universe....

Your body is a pillar of light.

Opening Up Your Energy Centers

Meditation is simple. In fact, one of the most difficult things about it is that it is so simple. Most people tend to think it should be more difficult or involve more effort...and so they don't think they are doing it correctly, and they quit doing it.

Active meditations like these involve a very subtle energy, directed by the imagination. Don't work at it too hard; play with it and have fun with it. You'll find it's easy to create experiences in your inner field of vision — and once you do, you start to see the results of those inner visions in the outer world. You'll remember these inner guided voyages as vividly as you remember all the other experiences in your life.

Here's another meditation, based on a simple truth that many people don't realize. If it were understood by more people, it would have a great effect on the world. This understanding in itself can be a direct path, something that can help you take quantum leaps in your evolution.

We have the power within us — in our mind, our imagination — to open up and activate every energy center in our body. Our bodies have many different energy centers, of course — *chakra* is the Sanskrit word for these energy centers — and in most people, one or more is blocked somewhat, so that energy isn't really moving freely through the whole being. Most people tend to focus their physical and emotional energy on one or two centers, simply out of habit and early conditioning.

In the traditional teachings of India, there are seven major chakras, and several minor ones. In the traditional teachings of the West (such as Kabbala), five major energy centers are described. It doesn't matter specifically how you choose to break them down. The teaching is essentially the same, at its roots.

Each chakra is a physical and emotional center of energy; each one corresponds to a major hormonal gland in the body. It's worthwhile to take the time to explore each one of them. There's a good chance that you've been ignoring a few, or holding a lot of tension and stress in them, which can lead to physical and emotional problems if that tension isn't released.

Try this meditation, and see what happens:

Sit comfortably, preferably with your spine straight. Or lie horizontally, if you prefer. Get comfortable, and relax....

Feel your presence, your life energy within....

Imagine a light above your head, touching the top of your head — a radiant, glowing ball of light energy that is at the open crown of your head and extends throughout the universe....

Imagine that this light is relaxing, soothing, healing the top of your skull, and the upper reaches of your phenomenal brain....

Imagine the whole area opening up, releasing and relaxing....

Imagine it opening up the whole universe....

Breathe deeply into this area....

Feel the breaths opening, cleansing, releasing, allowing the energy to circulate freely.

Now feel the light moving down into the center of your brain....

With closed eyes, look at the bright light between your brows, in your third eye....

Imagine a radiant, glowing ball of light energy fills your entire head, radiating outward....

Imagine this light relaxing, soothing, and healing the entire area....

Breathe deeply into your head....

Feel the breaths opening, cleansing, releasing, allowing the energy to circulate freely.

Now feel the light move down again and center in your throat....

Imagine a radiant, glowing ball of energy radiating outward....

Imagine that this light is relaxing, soothing, healing the entire area of your throat....

Breathe deeply into this area....

Feel the breaths opening, cleansing, releasing, allowing the energy to circulate freely....

Now feel the light move down again, and center in your heart....

Imagine a radiant, glowing ball of warm energy radiating out from your heart....

Imagine that this light is relaxing, soothing, healing the entire area of your heart and lungs and chest and back....

Breathe deeply into this area....

Feel the breaths opening your lungs and heart, cleansing, releasing, allowing the energy to circulate freely, throughout your entire body....

Open up your heart!

Now feel the light moving down again, and centering in your solar plexus and stomach area....

Imagine a radiant, glowing ball of spiritual energy radiating outward from your solar plexus and stomach....

Imagine that this light is relaxing, soothing, healing the entire area, including all internal organs....

Breathe deeply into this area....

Feel the breaths opening, cleansing, releasing, allowing the energy to circulate freely....

Now feel the light moving down again and centering in your sexual organs....

Imagine a glowing ball of radiant energy filling your whole sexual area....

Imagine the light is relaxing, soothing, healing the entire area....

Breathe deeply into this area....

Feel the breaths opening, cleansing, releasing, allowing the energy to circulate freely....

Now feel the light moving down again, and centering at the very base of your spine — your root chakra — then expanding down your legs and through your feet, into the earth....

Imagine a glowing ball of radiant energy radiating through the whole area....

Imagine that this light is relaxing, soothing, healing....

Breathe deeply into this area....

Feel the breaths opening, cleansing, releasing, allowing the energy to circulate freely....

Now feel the radiant light flowing through all your energy centers....

Feel the soothing power of the light that bathes your whole body....

Become aware that the light can charge any of your centers that have become depleted or blocked....

You are now recharging your energy centers....

See if you feel any tension in any area....

If you do, send light to it, and breathe into it.

You can affirm something like, *"I am releasing...I am relaxing...I am letting go of all tension, all obstacles...."*

Focus the light anywhere you wish....

Breathe into it, for as long as you wish....

Open up your energy centers!

Once you become aware of these energy centers in your body, you can direct the energy any way you wish. You are no longer at the mercy of forces beyond you, whether you feel they're outside forces or internal ones. You are the master of your being — you can choose where to focus your energies.

You can direct the course of your destiny, consciously. You are already doing it unconsciously, so you might as well do it consciously.

Creative Meditation

You don't have to *come to believe* anything about these kinds of meditations. Simply try one, and you will see its effects. Active, creative meditation demonstrates the fact that any image or belief that we hold in our subconscious mind will manifest in some way for us in the world. If we repeatedly tell ourselves that we're going to get some serious disease from eating junk food, for instance, we'll get some serious disease from eating junk food.

If we tell ourselves that we can't do something, we won't be able to do it. And if we tell ourselves, repeatedly, that we are now on our way to creating a far better life for ourselves, we will be successful.

Our bodies and the circumstances of our lives are the results of the conditioning we have accepted on deep, subconscious levels. It is not all that difficult to affect our subconscious thought processes, and even to change them deeply. All it takes is repeated affirmation, repeated visualization, repeated positive thought.

If there's something in your life you would like to change, something you're discontented with, try a creative meditation similar to the one that follows. It may have a powerful effect on your life the first time you do it; the best way to see some positive changes is to do something like this meditation (always feel free to adapt as you will) almost daily for at least three weeks.

What you are asking for may require some focused action in the world in addition to your meditation — very few people have made fortunes, for example, by sitting quietly and visualizing it and doing nothing else. But by doing this kind of creative meditation, you will find yourself receiving guidance from your own intuitive master — guidance that will tell you exactly what you need to do to achieve whatever you desire.

Do the following meditation — and then stay as open as possible to the ideas, impulses, hunches that come to you as a result of it.

Get comfortable...close your eyes...relax....

Take a deep breath, and as you exhale, affirm, "*My body is now relaxing deeply....*"

Take another deep breath, and as you exhale, affirm, "*My mind is now relaxing deeply....*"

Take one more deep breath, and as you exhale, affirm, "*I am letting everything go....*"

Feel your presence, your life energy, within....

Bathe in it, relax in it....

It feels so good to deeply relax....

Now imagine, in whatever way you can in your creative mind, exactly what you want to create for yourself in your life....

See and feel yourself doing it, being it, having it as clearly as you can, in as detailed a manner as you can....

Feel yourself expanding to be able to do it, be it, or have it in an easy and relaxed manner, a healthy and positive way....

Feel and see all obstacles falling away....

See yourself living the life of your dreams....

Make up affirmations that tell your subconscious mind that you are now on your way to creating what you want....

> **I am now creating the life of my dreams,**
> **in an easy and relaxed manner,**
> **a healthy and positive way,**
> **in its own perfect time,**
> **for the highest good of all.**

Take a moment to simply enjoy having what you want in life....

Give thanks for it....

Finish by saying to yourself,

> **This, or something better,**
> **is now manifesting**
> **in totally satisfying and harmonious ways**
> **for the highest good of all.**
> **So be it. So it is.**

Do this meditation as many times as it takes to feel you are carrying it deeply within you in some way throughout your day. Do it enough times to remember it.

Perhaps at first you will simply *feel* a change, without experiencing anything in the outer world. Then you may get an idea, think of something to do, or someone to contact. And soon, if you have repeated your visualization long enough for your subconscious to get it deeply, and prepare for it, the door of opportunity will open for you, and you will achieve whatever your heart has desired.

Ask and you shall receive.

Meditations on Our Three Bodies

The three meditations below contain a great many deep truths — if you have eyes to see. It has become common to talk of our four bodies, or states of being — physical, mental, emotional, and spiritual. This is a valuable concept to understand, and we'll look at it in more depth in the next chapter.

But there is another, powerful way to look at it. Many traditions, from both the East and the West — such as Buddhism and Kabbala — teach that we have *three* bodies, and this, too, is a valuable thing to understand, because understanding it can deeply affect our thoughts, our behavior, and the quality of our lives in general. The following has many correspondences to the description of the creation process we saw in chapter 2.

Our first body is the physical body — the body we can see, feel, and touch with our five outer, physical senses. It is the physical plane (called the *nirmanakaya* in Tibetan Buddhism). Here is the first meditation:

> Sit or lie comfortably, close your eyes, and relax....
>
> Relax from head to toe as you breathe out....
>
> Relax your mind, let all thought go as you breathe out....
>
> Let everything go....
>
> It feels really good to deeply relax....
>
> Tune into your physical body....
>
> Observe your breathing....
>
> Feel your heart beat....
>
> Notice how your body continues to operate perfectly, without any conscious attention on your part....
>
> Notice how it takes effortless care of itself, ever healing, ever renewing....
>
> There is nothing to reject about our physical bodies....
>
> They are precious beyond words....

They are a miracle of creation....

Affirm something like,

I am in perfect health physically.
Every day, in every way,
I am getting better and better.

Our second body is a very light, shimmering body that some people call our energy body. It is the life energy that fills every cell of our being. It is life itself — without it, our precious physical body becomes a decaying pile of garbage.

Our energy body is created by our thoughts and feelings, whether consciously or unconsciously. It is called the astral body in some Western traditions and the *sambhoga kaya* in Buddhism.

Sit or lie comfortably, close your eyes, and relax....

Relax from head to toe as you breathe out....

Relax your mind, let all thought go as you breathe out....

Let everything go....

It feels really good to deeply relax....

Now feel the energy within you, call it what you will....

You can call it your Presence, or your Being....

You can call it your energy body or astral body....

It is the body that is created with mind and emotion....

It is the body with the finer, inner senses of the imagination and inner vision and other inner intuitive
senses....

It is the body we can create for ourselves consciously in
our mind's inner eye....

It is what enables us to create anything we wish, in our
imagination....

It is on this plane of imagination and inner vision that
magic happens....

It is where the things we wish to create take form....

It is the plane on which creation takes place...before
anything is manifest on the physical plane, it must first
be imagined within us....

Enjoy your wonderful astral body....

Play with it like a child....

Travel anywhere in your imagination....

Create any kind of life for yourself that you want....

Give yourself total freedom....

Imagine yourself as radiantly healthy, strong, beautiful....

Imagine yourself doing exactly what you dream of doing....

Create in your mind, with a relaxed body, anything your heart desires....

Affirm your dreams are coming to be....

End with something like,

> **In an easy and relaxed manner,**
> **a healthy and positive way,**
> **in its own perfect time,**
> **for the highest good of all I pray....**
>
> **This, or something better,**
> **is now manifesting,**
> **in totally satisfying and harmonious ways,**

for the highest good of all.
So be it. So it is.

Notice how you feel as you finish your astral journey. This inner plane is much more than whimsical imaginings that have no effect on the physical world. It is *creative* imagination, for it literally creates the forms on very subtle planes of existence that will, in time, if we're persistent, become manifest on the physical plane in full three-dimensional form that we can see, touch, and feel.

You don't even have to worry *how* the things you are creating in your mind are going to manifest. Just keep picturing what you want, keeping the end result in mind. Soon the means to achieve that end will come to you — perhaps in a dream, or at the moment you wake up from sleep, or in a moment of insight, or in a daydream.

Then the steps will become clear to you. Accomplishing anything is just one simple step after another: a phone call, an appointment, writing a page, doing a blog, creating a brochure or website. Keep visualizing your goal — which just means keep *remembering* your goal — and trust your intuition to lead you to it.

We are all creative magicians, and the power of creation is within us, in the vast, limitless inner world of thought.

Our third body is the highest and most magnificent body of all: It is the body that encompasses all, the body that links us with the entire universe, the all-embracing body, called the spiritual body or the *dharma kaya* — the "body of truth" — in Tibetan Buddhism.

Sit or lie comfortably, close your eyes, and relax....

Relax from head to toe as you breathe out....

Relax your mind, let all thought go as you breathe out....

Let everything go....

It feels really good to deeply relax....

Be silent....

Feel, tune into, the wholeness of you....

You are a part of, and absolutely one with, the whole of the universe....

Focus on your highest spiritual nature....

It is the source of creation....

It is who you are, ultimately....

Pick any of the following words that are particularly resonant for you, and sit with them in silence:

I am the Ultimate Truth, beyond all words....

I am Absolute Reality....

I am Christ Consciousness....

I am Buddha Nature....

I am the one mind....

I am shimmering emptiness...the creative void...the ever-empty yet full seed of creation....

I am what is....

I am part of the quantum field....

I am part of the unity of every created thing....

I am the beyond....

I am That; That is all there is....

I am the Source....

I am my own true being....

I am my highest self....

I am the Kingdom of Heaven....

I am pure bliss....

I am Oneness....

Now, again, just sit in silence....

Take your time coming out of this deep meditation. Just sit in silence, savoring and nurturing all three of your wondrous bodies.

Be with Yourself

In case I lost you on that last meditation, we'll come back to something very simple — child's play, in fact. A very effective form of creative meditation is just to open yourself up to the ideas, fantasies, and impulses that come to you naturally when you're alone — whether you're walking, sitting, playing, even doing many types of work. It couldn't be simpler:

Take some time to be with yourself....

Take some time to just sit and do nothing for a while....

There's a story about Abraham Lincoln that I heard when I was a child and never forgot: One time, Abe and his brothers were supposed to be splitting rails for a fence around their land. But Abe kept wandering out into the woods and sitting there doing nothing, lost in his thoughts. Finally, Abe's brothers went to their father and complained, saying that Abe wasn't getting any work done. Abe's father must have been a wise man, because he said to his sons, "Just let him be...sometimes a person needs time to think."

Take time for yourself, every once in a while, to slow down and relax. Just lie on your bed for a while. Or sit with a plant, a tree....Or lie on your back and stare up at the clouds, like you used to do when you were young....

Watch a river flow...watch a flower grow...and you watch your life flow...and you see yourself grow...and you see Life itself... and you awaken your intuitive understanding....

> **Look up into a clear night's sky**
> **When you can see**
> **For a billion light-years**
>
> **Then you can see**
> **Infinity**
> **Beyond our smiles and tears**

Closing the Gates

This is one of the very first meditation practices I ever did, taught by my first yoga teacher, and I've never forgotten it. It can have a deep effect, if you let it.

Sit comfortably, with your spine straight....

Take a moment to relax....

Close your eyes, and take several deep breaths, rhythmically, relaxing more with every breath....

Now raise your hands up to your face, palms facing you....

Place your left thumb over your left ear and your right thumb over your right ear, shutting off the sound as effectively and as comfortably as possible....

Gently place your forefingers over your eyelids, blocking out external light as effectively and comfortably as possible....

Take a deep breath, and block your nostrils with your next finger....

Then, place your ring finger and little finger over your mouth....

You have now "closed the gates"....

Sit in silence and observe....

When you need to breathe, let go of the fingers blocking your nose, and breathe comfortably as you keep closing the gates with your other fingers....

Sit in silence and observe.

Usually I don't try to describe the results of a practice like this too specifically, because everyone's experience is different. But the first time I did this, I had a remarkable experience, and later I put it into these words:

The effect was wondrous. I was plunged into a vast inner space — as vast as oceans. Suddenly, there were whole new worlds to explore...worlds I had dreamed of when I was a kid, but had forgotten...worlds of magic...worlds of the mind, created in an instant by the mind.

I had found the key to something essential, something that changed the course of my life.

Mantras

A mantra is a chant, a repeated spoken word or series of words. There is no difference, essentially, between affirmations and mantras, and between prayers and mantras. Some mantras are short and simple, some are complex; some are in Sanskrit, some are in English and other languages. Pick any that feel good to you. They are a powerful way to reprogram our conscious and subconscious mind.

Sit quietly and comfortably for a moment....

Relax your body from head to toe....

Let everything go....

Feel your vibrant presence within....

Pick a phrase, or mantra, or affirmation, to focus on and to repeat....

Repeat it with feeling, until you experience it....

Some examples are:

Om Mani Padme Hum

(Or, in English)
I am the jewel of bliss
In the lotus of consciousness

OM

We know who we are, we are one

Sri Ram, Jai Ram, Jai Jai Rama

Be in peace

The kingdom of Heaven is within

Om namo Shivaya

I am free...I am strong...I am one with the Universe

Every day, in every way, I am getting better and better

May the longtime sun shine upon us
All love surround us
And the pure light within us
Guide our way home

The light of God surrounds us
The love of God enfolds us
The power of God flows through us
Wherever I am, God is, and all is well

The last chant, above, is a prayer of protection, especially suitable for any times you feel fearful or vulnerable.

Yoga and Tantra

This entire book is actually about yoga — yoga for the West. There have been many books written about yoga — but then, it is a vast subject, and it is continually evolving.

Some teachers of tantra in the Eastern tradition separate tantra from yoga, saying there is the path of yoga and the path of tantra and that the two are directly opposite. But I don't look at it that way. As I understand it, tantra is a form of yoga, a way of life that encompasses every possible form of yoga. To put it succinctly:

Tantra is the yoga
of every moment of your life.

The practice of tantra is the yoga of those who are ready for a much broader definition of both yoga and tantra.

Yoga in its broadest and deepest root-word sense means "union," which is basically the same root-word meaning as *religion*, which means "reuniting." The practice of yoga ultimately leads to a deep realization of your union with the Universe, with your highest spiritual self and greatest purpose in life.

The root word of *tantra* means "to weave" — for tantra is the stuff of life, the fabric of our lives, including every moment, every experience. Tantra yoga is a rapid and powerful path:

Tantra is the awareness that leads to
finding our highest expression —
love, fulfillment, freedom, enlightenment —
within every moment of daily life, rejecting nothing.

Every moment we are studying tantra. And every moment we are doing yoga, in the broadest sense of the word.

Still, it is very useful and healthful at times to do specific yoga practices. I'll describe a few forms — traditional and nontraditional — that have been particularly good for me.

Hatha Yoga

Hatha yoga is the traditional series of physical practices that most people associate with the word *yoga*. Many teachers also include *pranayama,* or breathing exercises, and meditation along with the study of hatha yoga. There are a great many fine teachers of hatha yoga around, nearly everywhere. And there are a lot of great books, audios, and videos on the subject.

The best hatha yoga exercises are nonstrenuous (in my opinion), and they are very good for body, mind, emotions, and spirit. Doing yoga has an immediate effect: strengthening, healing, and calming. (But don't beat yourself up if you miss your yoga session!)

Kum Nye

There is a very effective form of physical yoga I learned at a Tibetan center and is now taught in many different places and being incorporated into a great many different forms of therapy and healing in the West. The Tibetans call it *kum nye,* or "body relaxation."

You can do it yourself, unassisted, or you can do it with others as well.

Simply relax for a moment...take a few deep breaths....

Tune into your body...feel the energy within...feel if there is any tension within....

Now simply start poking, probing, and rubbing your body (or your friend's body) wherever you feel tension....

You can, if you wish, start at the head and neck, and work down....

Or you can start with any area of tension....

Explore your body, gently yet firmly....

Search for tightness and tension — especially in your neck, shoulders, and chest....

And in your stomach area, and under your ribs....

When you find a tense spot, tune into it and massage it deeply....

Send it a warm, deep, loving, healing energy....

Imagine it dissolving, releasing....

Breathe deeply into it, and feel it release....

Do whatever you need to do physically to release it....

You may want to make sounds, or move in a certain way....

Let your breath, sound, and movement dissolve that tension....

Just visualize it dissolving, and let it go....

Finish by just relaxing and breathing quietly.

Sometimes — especially in your neck and shoulder area, and in your feet, and along the bones of your lower legs — you can actually feel the tension in the form of a small lump or "crystal." It may in fact actually be crystallized energy that is blocked in your body. By rubbing deeply into these crystals, and imagining them releasing as you exhale deeply, you can sometimes feel them dissolving, and feel a release, a lightening up of the tension you are carrying.

One very nice feeling technique is to rub the earlobes from top to bottom in a stroking manner between your thumb and forefinger. It is very relaxing; it's even good for getting kids to sleep.

If you do this practice, you'll feel your tension releasing; it is in our power to dissolve all unnecessary tension in our bodies. For our tension, too, is empty, like everything else. It, too, is pure energy, pure light, in constant movement....

Free-Form Yoga

This practice — a form of nontraditional yoga — can take just a very short time. It is simple, and it is healing, physically and emotionally. Give it a try.

Stand up (or lie down if you feel like it), take a deep breath, and, as you exhale, relax your body....

Take another deep breath and, as you exhale, relax your mind, letting all thought go....

Take another deep breath, and look within....

Feel your presence, your life energy....

Now focus your attention on your feelings....

Let go of thought in your head and focus on your gut feelings....

Take another breath, and move more deeply into your feelings....

Start to breathe, and to move, slowly or rapidly, depending on what you're feeling....

Maybe you just want to breathe deeply, and stay physically still....

Or maybe you want to move....

Just follow your feelings....

Don't think about what you're doing at all.... As soon as you find yourself thinking about it, drop down into

your feelings again, and just move in any way that feels
good.

Absolutely any type of movement — including stillness
— is allowed, and encouraged....

Do whatever you have the energy to do for as long as
you want to do it....

Do it for just a minute or two, or for an hour — as long as it
lasts. Use it to release, to relax, to take a break, to stretch your
body...to yawn, to lie still, to dance...to jump, to fly, to slowly
stretch...maybe to yell or shout, or shake your body vigorously....Do whatever movement your body wants to do.

This is a very effective form of meditation and yoga. It gets you
into your feelings and out of your head...into your intuitive
body/mind and out of your rational mind. And it exercises,
heals, releases tensions, and opens you up to receiving energy
from the ever-abundant Universe.

The Way Is Infinite

Eckhart Tolle summed it up nicely (as he is wont to do). When
he was asked about meditation, all he said was,

**Don't let your meditation
get in the way of your meditation.**

And Alan Watts put it in a book title:

This is it.

This is it. This is your meditation. This moment. This is the direct path of tantra.

There is a season for everything....

A time for discipline...a time to let discipline go.

A time for searching...a time to stop searching.

A time to read and study...a time not to read or study.

A time to go to workshops, group meditations, and gatherings ...and a time not to go.

A time to get into growth-oriented or spiritual or artistic or scientific or business activity...and a time to get out of it.

A time to have a teacher...and a time to be your own teacher.

The Way is Infinite.

Everyone has their own path — endless variations on the same theme. We are all endlessly growing in wisdom and compassion, endlessly expanding toward freedom and perfection. It is our nature. We are a vital part of an endlessly evolving universe.

11

Aging and Healing

**We have the power to rebuild ourselves anew,
if we but awaken to the power of
our creative visualization.**

We live in a culture that extols the virtues of youth and has forgotten the value of old age. Being young and vital is a wonderful thing, and it deserves to be celebrated and enjoyed. And yet, as we start to age, there is no need to reject it in any way. Aging is part of a great natural process, and every step of that process has its own beauty and perfection.

A Youthful Observation

When I was in my midteens, my father was approaching fifty. One day two friends of his came by to visit. They had all gone to high school together and were the same age. But as I looked at the three of them together, I was struck by something that I knew was very significant, but I didn't know why at the time. Only years later did it make sense.

One of my father's friends looked and moved like an old man, slow and stiff, and the other looked like a young man, healthy, strong, filled with youthful energy. My father looked about his age — somewhere between the two.

I asked myself, repeatedly, why these two men of the same age looked to be such different ages. One could have been the other's father! It didn't make sense to me at the time — because I was assuming that aging was a process that occurs at the same rate for all people. But these two men were obviously aging at different rates. One was old, one was young.

A few years later, my father told me that the old-looking one had died. I wasn't surprised. The young-looking man was active, creative, healthy, and worked full-time well into his later years.

The Aging Process

There are several processes — physical, emotional, and mental — that powerfully affect our aging.

Physically, our diet and exercise certainly affect our rate of aging. I am not a total pure-foods advocate by any means, but it's obvious that if people abuse their bodies by eating too much, drinking too much, and not getting enough exercise, then their bodies are naturally going to start slowing down and developing problems.

Our emotional and mental processes also powerfully affect our rate of aging, for we are constantly giving our bodies operating instructions with our minds and feelings. These instructions are usually on a subconscious level, so we aren't aware of them. But we can easily become conscious of them — all we need to do is focus the light of our inner observation on what we're telling ourselves and what we're feeling, and the subconscious patterns emerge and become clear.

If we're telling ourselves — consciously and repeatedly so it becomes accepted and absorbed by our subconscious minds — that we're young and strong and healthy, we're going to stay young and strong and healthy. If we're telling ourselves that we're weak, or prone to sickness, or fat, or old, or whatever, we're going to continue to create that for ourselves.

Be aware of what you tell yourself!

Think Yourself Thin

A lot of people have difficulty seeing how this process works. So let's take weight as an example. Imagine that you're five-foot-five and weigh three hundred pounds. You've put so much fat on your body that you have difficulty moving. Why are you so overweight? Many people believe it's because of hormonal imbalances — and that's sometimes true, but the imbalance is an *effect* of something deeper and not the root cause of the problem.

A large part of the problem is the amount of food you are putting into your body: You are taking in more calories than you're burning. Yet a lot of overweight people claim they eat less than thin people — why is this? Many say it's their metabolism — some people are blessed with an active metabolism that quickly digests calories, and others are unfortunate enough to have a slow metabolism that surrounds them in fat. "Oh, everything I eat goes right to my thighs," I've heard people say. (Watch what you say! Your words are powerful instructions to your subconscious mind.)

It's true that people have different rates of metabolism, but again it is not the root cause of your condition. *Why* is your metabolism sluggish while that of others is more active? Certainly your physical activity affects your metabolism. One good way to lose weight is to get more exercise. But something else is an even deeper root cause of fat: *It is what you're telling yourself, repeatedly*, that is determining how much weight you're holding on to.

If you're constantly telling yourself, "I'm fat" or "This food is making me fat," your body will follow these instructions and create exactly the body that you are imagining for yourself.

If, on the other hand, you start telling yourself, repeatedly in the mornings and throughout the day, that you are becoming slim and healthy, your body will start responding to these instructions, and the weight will start coming off. (It helps to eat fewer doughnuts, too.)

Say you weigh three or four hundred pounds. Obviously, you've been telling yourself you are fat. If you start repeatedly telling yourself you are losing weight, becoming slimmer and slimmer, no matter how ridiculous it may seem to you, no matter how irrational, you are going to create some changes for yourself.

The first changes will be subtle. Now that you're telling yourself that you're getting thinner, your posture is going to improve. You'll start carrying all your weight more easily, and you'll feel lighter, even though you're still breaking the bathroom scale. If you stay with affirmations like "I am now becoming slim; I am beautiful" throughout the day, for several weeks, especially every time you catch yourself telling yourself otherwise, your body will gradually conform to your consistent thoughts, as it always does. It will take some time, but gradually, you will think yourself thin. Or beautiful. Or younger. Or whatever your heart desires.

Why not? You deserve it! It's certainly worth a try...and it's a lot cheaper and easier than dieting. (I don't mean to put dieting down, for diets can obviously help people lose weight. Yet the most important thing to look at in a diet is whether it helps you change your thoughts so that you're changing the subconscious programming you're giving yourself.)

If these affirmations don't work for you, you might very well have some deep emotional reasons for wanting or needing to be fat that you will need to examine and deal with. As you become more aware of your deep feelings, you can find the right words, the right affirmations — the right operating instructions — that can counteract these feelings, and then the weight will dissolve as your emotional blocks do.

A Powerful Practice

Take a clear, objective look at your body, right at this moment....

Is it fat? Thin? Strong? Weak? Beautiful? Ugly? Old? Young? Lethargic? Active? Sagging? Firm?

Describe your body to yourself....

Now reflect on the fact that your body is the concrete physical result of years of emotional and mental conditioning that you have been giving yourself...or that you have accepted from someone else without questioning or denying it....

Make up some affirmations that mentally describe the type of body you want....

Say these affirmations, with emotional force and certainty — this can powerfully help program your subconscious mind, even if part of you thinks they're ridiculous and false....

Whenever you run into any kind of inner resistance, overcome it with another positive affirmation....

Wait, with a bit of patience, and see what happens — inevitably, positive changes will occur, if you keep repeating your affirmations.

These kinds of affirmations are sometimes difficult for people to accept, because it can seem as if you are blatantly lying to yourself. And in a way, it's true — but you're lying for a good cause, and it will have a good effect.

In order for us to create anything, we must first imagine it mentally and feel it emotionally, creating an inner experience of the reality we want to create next.

**Our affirmations are creating the blueprints
for our future evolution.**

Create a Healthy, Beautiful Body

I once knew a woman who was well into middle age but had the looks and skin tone of a teenager. I asked her what her secret was, and she said, "It's in the family. My mother has great skin tone; so does my sister." Because she had been affirming that all her life, instead of worrying about losing her tone (and putting energy into creating just what she was afraid of), she had created a toned, beautiful body.

There are many techniques for creating a healthy body. Simple affirmations alone will do it — make up your own. There are other techniques as well, such as the two that follow, first a short version, then a longer one:

Short version:
Sit, or lie down, in a comfortable position....

Take a few breaths, and relax your body, your mind, and your entire being....

Now simply imagine a field of light enveloping you....

Your whole body is bathed in a healing light....

Now imagine your ideal body, strong and beautiful, however you wish to see it....

Imagine that you are drawing that body to you, and merging with it, and becoming it....

Imagine your physical body perfectly conforming to your newly created light body, so that your physical body is actually changing, growing strong and more beautiful....

Focus the light of your mind's eye on any area of your body where you want special change, special attention....

Create the body you wish in your mind's eye, and know that you are on your way to creating it physically....

Find an affirmation or two to complete the process....

Perhaps *"I am young and strong,"* or *"My body is growing stronger, and more beautiful every day,"* or *"Every day, in every way, I am getting better and better...."*

Get up, stretch, and feel younger and stronger and healthier and more beautiful.

Longer version:
Take a deep breath, and relax your body deeply from head to toe as you exhale....

Take another deep breath, and relax your mind, and let all thought go....

Sit in silence and stillness for a while....

Now, if you wish, you can go through the meditation we did in the last chapter (page 165) for opening up your energy centers...or you can just continue here:

Feel the light inside your body....

Now move that light through your entire body, awakening each center of energy within you....

Imagine your body to be a glowing, vibrating light body....

Imagine that it is elastic and changeable....

With the power of your creative imagination, run energy through your whole body, directed by your mind's eye....

Now focus on your feet, and imagine energy moving up your left side (or your right side, if that feels better) to the top of your head, then down your other side to your feet, then up again....

Do this a few times....

Then run the energy from your feet up your back to the top of your head, then down the front of your body and back to your feet again....

Do this a few times, too, imagining that the light energy is cleansing, refreshing, rebuilding your entire body....

Then run energy from your feet straight up the center of your body, all the way to the top of your head....

Let it shower over your whole body, bathing you in a fountain of vibrant light energy....

Then gather it up at your feet again and bring it up your spine again....

Do this a few times, imagining that you are bathing yourself in the elixir of life, the fountain of youth....

Now you've awakened your whole physical, emotional, mental, and spiritual system with the power of your energy directed by your mind....Now you can direct this energy to any part of your body you want, healing, rejuvenating, rebuilding your body as you wish....

Feel your energy building new muscle, tightening your skin tone, dissolving tension....

Feel your energy creating exactly the type of body you wish.

Create the body you want in your mind's eye. Your physical form will soon follow. James Allen said it beautifully in his classic book *As You Think* (written over a century ago):

"The body is the servant of the mind. It obeys the operations of the mind, whether they be deliberately chosen or automatically expressed. At the bidding of unhealthy thoughts the body sinks rapidly into disease and decay; at the command of glad and beautiful thoughts, it becomes clothed with youthfulness and beauty....

**"The body is a delicate and plastic instrument,
and responds readily to the thoughts
by which it is impressed."**

It's extraordinary just how quickly our physical bodies respond to our thoughts. Keep picturing yourself as young, vibrant, healthy. At the same time, however, love and appreciate the phenomenal body you have at this moment, and all the other gifts you have been given. There is a perfection in everyone, at every moment. This is the teaching of tantra.

Nurture All Your States of Being

Earlier we talked about our four bodies, or levels of being: physical, mental, emotional, and spiritual. This is a wonderful thing to understand, and it is very powerful to affirm,

**I am in perfect health,
physically, mentally, emotionally,
and spiritually.**

I met a ninety-year-old man who told me that single affirmation was the secret to his lifelong health. Are you affirming that you are in good physical, mental, and emotional health? (We don't really need to affirm we're in good spiritual health, because our spiritual nature is perfect and whole.)

Are you nurturing your physical, mental, emotional, and spiritual states of being? Are you balanced, fully aware of each of your different levels of being? So many people become strongly identified with one or two of their bodies and ignore the others. There are the purely physical people who ignore their emotions or mental development, the emotional people who ignore their physical and mental bodies, and the intellectuals who are oblivious to their physical bodies and their emotional states. All these states are unbalanced.

We are physical, emotional, mental, and spiritual beings. Cherish and treasure and nourish every one of your miraculous, powerful bodies. I've written something very similar to this in another book, but it's worth repeating:

> **You have everything you need:**
> **a miraculous physical and emotional body,**
> **a phenomenal mind,**
> **and a vast and powerful connection**
> **to the whole of creation.**
> **Now it's just a matter of focusing them**
> **in the right direction.**

The Principles of Healing

Healing is an organic, natural process that can occur on any of our four levels of being. Our bodies are healing themselves all the time, cleansing, purifying, repairing damage. Our bodies are designed to function easily, effortlessly, and without pain. Pain is simply a message to us that something needs to be changed.

Our bodies are always healing themselves, as long as we aren't blocking the process or actually desiring the sickness on some deep level because there's a payoff in it for us — a break from too much activity, or sympathy, attention, love, or getting out of an uncomfortable situation. Your body is designed to be perfectly healthy. If it isn't, focus on one or more of the following levels of being:

Physical level:
Take time to relax your body, and let the body's natural healing processes occur, with as little interference from you as possible....

Rest and relax as much as possible....

If the affected part of your body is too cool, warm it up; if it is too warm, cool it off; if it is too dry, keep it moist; if it is too wet, keep it dry....

Basically, just relax, eat simple, good food, drink a lot of fluids, and give your body time to heal itself....

Emotional level:
Don't resist being sick — accept it....Accept what is....

Your body needs to rest, so give it time to relax....

Accept all your feelings...express them to a sympathetic friend....

Ask yourself honestly, and repeatedly if necessary, what you are feeling emotionally that is contributing to your disease....

Have you been feeling resentful?...
Have you been feeling burned out at work and in need of a break?...

Have you been feeling that you can't express yourself to others?...

Often, just giving yourself permission to fully express your feelings can dissolve sickness at the root....

Mental level:
What do you truly think is the cause of your illness or disease?

A deep part of you knows the answer....

What is the root cause, beneath the physical symptoms?

Picture yourself strong and well....

Affirm that you are strong and well....

Spiritual level:
There is no disease. You are a perfect being....

Rise and walk and be strong and healthy....

Your faith, your understanding of what is, has made you whole....

Keep Growing

There's no need to grow *old* — simply grow, and keep growing. We will all age, but we can all be very young for our age. We are designed by nature to keep expanding our horizons, endlessly, becoming clearer, more aware, and more powerful with each passing year. Affirm this to be, and it will be!

12

Politics

**We have power, if we just
embrace that power.**

We saw these words by Abraham Isaac Kook, renowned Torah
scholar, at the beginning of this book:

**The higher the truth,
the simpler it is.**

The great, guiding truths of our lives can be stated very simply. Look at the simplicity of Jesus's words: *Ask and you shall
receive....Love one another as I have loved you....Peter, put
away your sword — if you live by the sword, you die by the
sword.* How could these things have been said any more simply
or clearly? And each one is a key to a brighter life.

Pete Seeger, the famed American songwriter, gave us a simple
key to creating a harmonious society and world:

**It's a very important thing to learn
to talk to people you disagree with.**

That in itself is the key to peace on our planet in our lifetimes.

Native American traditions are old and deep; a great many of
the ideas of our democracy came from Native American ways.
In the 1700s, the founders of our democracy were well aware
of the confederacy of Native American tribes known as the Six
Nations, and parts of the agreement that peacefully bound the
tribes together influenced the drafting of the US Constitution.
What came to be known as the "Seven Generations" pledge
gives us some powerful truths clearly and simply:

> In all of your deliberations in the Confederate Council,
> in your efforts at law making, in all your official acts,
> self-interest shall be cast into oblivion.... Look and lis-
> ten for the welfare of the whole people and have always
> in view not only the present but also the coming gener-
> ations, even those whose faces are yet beneath the sur-
> face of the ground — the unborn of the future Nation.

When some Native American tribes meet in council, they sit in
a circle. It is understood by all that everyone has a voice and
a right to be heard. And it is understood that when any object
is placed in the center of the circle, everyone sees it differently,
because everyone has a different perspective. And when any idea
is placed in the center of the circle, everyone will have their own
opinion, based on their perspective, experience, and personality.

World politics would transform instantly if we adopted this one simple principle:

**Everyone deserves respect,
and everyone has a right to be heard.**

This is the only way we'll ever find lasting peace in the world. We need to sit in council with each other, giving everyone in the circle of humanity a voice. This is what it means to be a free person in a free society. We have a voice, we are respected, we have human rights, and we are free to do our best to lead the life of our dreams.

When we give others respect, we automatically start working in partnership with them. The only workable solution to the world's problems is to live and work in partnership with the whole family of humanity. It's not all that difficult to do, but it requires some changes in our habitual ways of relating to one another.

Here's another great truth that can be expressed very simply:

**The only way to a peaceful, prosperous future
is to live and work in partnership with others.**

The Land of the Free

The past several decades have witnessed a great change in the consciousness of people throughout the world. A deeper level of awareness has emerged, a greater sensitivity to the need for everyone globally to be respected and to have basic human rights, including rights of life, liberty, and the pursuit of happiness.

The ideal of a land of the free has spread throughout the world. We are truly free, if we embrace that freedom. In most of the world now, we're free to live the life of our dreams. The old social structures — which were often backed by force — have crumbled. You are free to be who you are, and do what you want, as long as you're not violating the rights of others. You can be single, married, straight, gay, bisexual, transgender, or anything else and, in most places in this new world that is emerging, your human rights will not be violated because of who you are and what you choose to do. You're free to live as you want to live.

We are finding new ways to live in the world, and new ways to relate to one another. This awakening comes at a critical time, for the old thinking that still dominates most governments, politics, and business as usual has created huge dinosaurs that are rapidly becoming extinct.

The culture as a whole, led by its most progressive thinkers and doers, is rediscovering its own intuitive, caring nature, which has been stifled, almost obliterated, by the culture of domination and exploitation that has ruled most cultures over the past few thousand years. But we are learning again to understand the power of partnership over the power of exploitation; we are learning to balance the rational with the intuitive. We are learning that science and politics don't have to reject the intuitive, the emotional, or the spiritual.

As this intuitive awareness began to rise again to the surface of the mass consciousness, there seemed to be a huge schism between the intuitive and the rational, between the spiritual and the political or scientific points of view. The infant intuitive force couldn't survive along with the fierce, intense energies of the political and scientific and so had to divorce itself from them, and nurture itself in private.

This intuitive awareness has now gained sufficient ground and strength that we're seeing a unique blending of the intuitive and the scientific, and of the spiritual and political. Actually, it isn't unique at all: Albert Einstein was an outspoken advocate of intuition in science, and Mahatma Gandhi successfully blended the spiritual and political many years ago — and Gandhi was in turn influenced by Emerson and Thoreau, highly progressive American writers in the early 1800s.

The schism is over. We no longer have to separate the spiritual and political. We no longer have to avoid certain areas of activity in order to protect our new awareness. The whole world is our playground and laboratory for the great experiment of our lives — the lives of a free people.

Your Personal Power

As creative, free individuals, we have a great deal of personal power to be put to good use, both spiritually and politically. History has proven that individuals do have a great deal of power politically, once they find skillful means to express that power.

Here is one hair-raising example: Daniel Ellsberg, a former Defense Department official, stated on national television that Nixon, when he was president, had a plan — appropriately called the "madman project" — to end the war in Vietnam in the same way the Korean War was ended: through threat of a nuclear attack that would be far more devastating than Hiroshima. The North Vietnamese were offered an ultimatum, backed up with nuclear power.

But, unlike North Korea, North Vietnam didn't accept the ultimatum. And, according to Ellsberg, Nixon was fully prepared to put the madman project into effect and get us into an atomic war. Fortunately, this coincided with a huge series of demonstrations against the war in which hundreds of thousands of people marched in Washington, DC, and other cities across the nation. Nixon realized that he didn't have the support of the American people and didn't put his well-named plan into effect.

So it was the American people — those who organized and marched, and those who spoke out in other ways — who avoided nuclear war. We have the power, if we but embrace it. And there are so many different creative channels through which we can express that power.

The Deep Meaning of Karma

The West is only now beginning to understand the meaning of the word *karma*. Even though it is a core teaching of Christianity as well as of Eastern teachers (*"As you sow, so you shall reap"*), somehow the concept of karma has been ignored and forgotten in the West. Our political leaders all too often have acted as though their negative actions would not have negative results.

Understanding the concept of karma is critical to having a good life. We must understand it and practice it, if we are going to continue to grow and be healthy as a society, and not crumble and decay.

The law of karma is simply the law of cause and effect: *For every action we put into the world, we receive an equal and appropriate reaction.* The law of karma explains why a thief will get ripped off, why an angry person lives in an angry world, and why a loving person lives in a loving world. We reap what we sow.

Karma operates in our lives individually, and it operates for the whole of humanity as well. The governments of the world's greatest powers have created enormous problems for the whole planet by being completely unconscious of the laws of karma. Any attempts by a government to dominate and control others create endless anger and resentment. Violence leads endlessly to more violence. We have it summed up nicely on a magnet on our refrigerator:

Mom was right.
Fighting doesn't solve anything.

It's time for all of us to change some basic attitudes. We must *all* — every nationality, every race, every group, with no exceptions — ask for personal, clear guidance, for the understanding that will show us the how to overcome our past mistakes, individually and collectively.

We must stop fighting others. There are more civilized ways to resolve problems.

We all must learn to forgive, and accept others. Everyone has a right to be here; everyone has a right to life, liberty, and the pursuit of happiness.

We must take responsibility for the abolition, within our lifetimes, of racism, sexism, starvation, poverty, and exploitation in our global community. It can be done, if we turn the power of our imaginations, the power of creative visualization, on these global issues.

Buckminster Fuller put it brilliantly. He offered this challenge to humanity more than fifty years ago: "To make the world work for 100 percent of humanity in the shortest possible time through spontaneous cooperation without ecological damage or disadvantage to anyone." He called this "The World Game," and he added these insights:

> For the first time in history it is now possible to take care of everybody at a higher standard of living than any have ever known. All humanity now has the option to become enduringly successful....

> Never forget that you are one of a kind. Never forget that if there weren't any need for you in all your uniqueness to be on this earth, you wouldn't be here in the first place. And never forget, no matter how overwhelming life's challenges and problems seem to be, that one person can make a difference in the world. In fact, it is always because of one person that all the changes that matter in the world come about. So be that one person.

The single most important thing to remember is the teaching of one of the greatest masters to influence the West, one who understood karma completely, and taught it, and lived it:

> **Love one another, as I have loved you....**
> **Do unto others as you would have them do unto you....**
> **As you sow, so shall you reap.**

We can all do something right now that has great power: We can make changes within ourselves. As more and more of us change our attitudes and behavior, more and more outer forms naturally emerge that help to solve the world's great problems. A great many powerful groups have emerged already that are changing the world for the better.

We live in exciting times, times of change and growth. Some people are embracing the changes enthusiastically. Some people resist all the signs of necessary change until they fall and perish for lack of adaptability. It all depends on your karma — on the things you have done, and the things you think and do today and tomorrow.

Politics in a New Age

None of us lives in a vacuum. Everything we do affects others. It is time to help create a politics that fully appreciates and balances the interests of all people. Old-age politics and old-age business practices are on their way out — dying from their own lack of vision and adaptability. By "old age" I mean any activity in which some people take unfair advantage of other people, where some are fattened to an extreme and others are deprived, where there is a win-lose relationship. At its extreme, old-age politics and business could lead to nuclear war — a total lose-lose proposition, fueled by insanity.

Politics in this new age creates win-win relationships that support everyone involved. There is no need to take advantage of anyone else. There is plenty for all, if we but see it, and create it. We can all live in abundance — every person on this planet — if we stop taking advantage of one another and work and live with respect for one another and for the planet that sustains us.

It can be done. It is already being done in many forms. It is up to each of us to create more of these forms, and to expand the existing forms until their impact is felt in the mass consciousness, and until we transform our world into a beautiful and supportive place for all.

So be it. So it is!

13

Enlightenment

You are, in truth, an unlimited being.
All you need to do is to see what you really are,
and you are enlightened.

The word *enlightenment*, like the word *tantra*, is used in so many different ways by so many different people that it becomes meaningless unless it is clearly defined and understood.

According to some traditions, enlightenment is the very top of the mountain of our ever-evolving consciousness, the culmination of lifetime after lifetime of searching and discovering — a peak so distant and remote for most people that only one person in each great age ever achieves real enlightenment.

In other traditions, enlightenment is a state that is possible for anyone to discover. According to Zen Buddhism, enlightenment is an experience that can come in a moment to anyone who is receptive to it. The *kensho* experience, as it is called, is a deep, even if sometimes momentary, experience of oneness, of bliss, of completeness that many, many people all over the world have had and continue to have.

The Bottom Line

The bottom line is this: Enlightenment is whatever you define it to be. You can believe that you will never achieve it — and you will never achieve it. You can believe that you will achieve it at some time in the future, when you finally get yourself together — and you may or may not create it for yourself in the future, depending on whether you change your belief and create it in the present moment. All teachings of the enlightenment experience point within us, showing us that enlightenment is our deepest, truest essence. It is not something we achieve; it is something we discover we had all along.

**All we need to do is to connect with our essence,
to see what really is,
and we are enlightened.**

A Tibetan teacher told me this story, and it describes the process and nature of enlightenment very well:

One night a woman had an intensely vivid dream, so vivid that she thought it was real. She dreamed that she lost her head, literally — her head was missing from her shoulders.

In the morning, she got up and frantically went searching for her head. She searched everywhere for it, and she could not find it. Her desperate cries for it didn't do any good at all.

Finally, she went to a teacher and asked where she could find her head. The teacher simply held up a mirror for her to see herself.

And she realized that she had it all along, and it was only in a dream that she lost it.

This story is a beautiful metaphor for the process and nature of enlightenment. The central character is a woman rather than a man — this symbolizes the intuitive within each of us, the fact that our enlightenment lies within our intuitive nature, the feminine principle within us rather than within our rational nature, which you could call the masculine principle within us.

Searching desperately for your intuitive nature will never reveal it to you. You must simply find someone or something that is a mirror for you — something that will reflect your true nature.

Look closely at yourself, and you will one day discover that all your limitations, all your shortcomings, are imaginary. You are, in truth, an unlimited being. Your body and mind are literally composed of light energy. You are enlightened, here and now. You always have been, and you always will be. Just see that this is so, and it is so.

This is a deep and wonderful teaching that has been given in many different words, in many different traditions, Eastern and Western. To put it simply:

We are much greater beings than we think we are. We have vast higher levels of consciousness that we rarely perceive, and most of us have forgotten them entirely, forgotten that they are part of who we are.

We all have a Christ consciousness, we all have a Buddha nature, within us. Our natural state of being is one of enlightenment.

You don't have to seek elsewhere for your answers; you don't have to look elsewhere for your greatest treasures. You find them within.

14

Daily Life

This is the direct path:
Turn every moment of your life
into a meditation.

Every moment of your life is your practice, if you want to look at it that way. You can call it the path of tantra; you can call it anything you want. It doesn't matter what words you use. Just grasp this idea:

Every moment of life is your meditation.

Whatever happens, whatever unfolds in front of you, is a vital part of your path.

When you get up and go to the bathroom, it can become a wonderful meditation that leads to great depth and serenity. Sit on the throne and feel the wonder of your being.

When you're eating breakfast, you're meditating. Feel the food and drink nurturing and strengthening your body and mind.

Feel the vibrant healing energy that moves through your body every moment of your life. Repeat the mantra *"Every day, in every way, I am getting better and better."* Or *"I am in perfect health, physically, mentally, emotionally, and spiritually."*

When you're sitting in traffic, you're meditating. You can reflect on the koan given by Suzuki Roshi at the San Francisco Zen Center: *How do I become enlightened while driving on the freeway?*

Every moment can become a moment of meditation. Turn an argument with someone into a meditation on your anger. Turn a moment of frustration with yourself into a meditation on your expectations and demands.

That's the direct path. It's different from anyone else's path — it's absolutely unique.

You are absolutely unique. And so your path is unique.

If you try to follow anyone, even a beloved teacher, and model your path after theirs, you will never reach your fullest potential.

You come to realize who you are only by knowing and accepting every bit of yourself, every moment, and fully being yourself every moment.

You will never be Jesus or Mother Teresa or Buddha or Pema Chödrön or Buckminster Fuller or Eckhart Tolle (to name a few great teachers at random). You can only be yourself every moment. Discover who you are, and you find your own unique path along the way.

We can call it tantra, we can call it the direct path, we can call it using skillful means, creative visualization, or anything else. It is the path of discovering your deepest dreams and desires, and realizing who you are in the fullest, deepest sense.

You are limitless. You are light. You are eternal.

You're a star!

Our Life and Our Life Situation

Great truths can be stated simply; Eckhart Tolle has the ability to clearly sum up something in a way that can immediately affect the quality of our lives. Every word he writes or says is pure tantra, if you look at it that way. Looking at every moment of our lives through the lens of his understanding can bring us love, fulfillment, freedom, and enlightenment. He once summed it up this way:

**We have our life,
and we have our life situation.**

Our life situation will always be exactly the way it is, filled with our life stories that so often have problems, difficulties, challenges. Life is tough. The world's a mess. That's undeniably true. But we don't have to get anxious or depressed about it if we just keep remembering that we have our *life*, as well as our life situation.

We are life itself, the energy of the universe endlessly creating itself. That is who we are.

When we realize that, we connect with that energy, we *are* that energy, and all our problems dissolve in an instant.

All we need to do is remember this:

**We are not our life situation
or our life story.
We are life itself.**

We are a shining, radiant field of light and love. We are a vast conscious awareness viewing the play of our lives from a place of peace, serenity, total acceptance, and, most of all, love, love, love.

15

Freedom

**You were meant to be as free as a bird,
or a star, or any master
who has walked this earth.**

Henry David Thoreau wrote this (I've slightly paraphrased):

**What is it to be born free,
and not to live free?
What is it to be free from England
and slaves to prejudice?...
It is our children's children
who might really be free.**

We are the children of Thoreau's children. Are we free yet? Or are we still creating our own prisons, because of the limitations of our own thoughts?

At the beginning of this book, we defined tantra in this way:

**Tantra is the awareness that every moment
is a direct path to love, freedom,
fulfillment, enlightenment.**

Every moment is the key. In this moment, we have within us the guidance to turn this moment into lightness, awareness, serenity.

A Final Practice: An Essential Key

Here's a final practice that can give you that essential key of connecting with your inner guidance and letting your own understanding guide you from now on, into a lighter, brighter life.

Sit, or lie down on your back, get comfortable....

Close your eyes, take a deep, cleansing breath....

As you exhale, relax from head to toe, letting all tension go....

Breathe in again deeply, and as you exhale, relax your mind and let all thought go....

Take a third deep, cleansing breath, and as you exhale....

Let everything go.

Now think of a problem area in your life....

Is there something you'd love to do, be, or have that isn't happening at the moment? Relax more deeply, from head to toe, as you think about the problem, or something you want to change....

Ask yourself, *"What is it about* _____ *that I need to understand?"* Put your problem in the blank space....

Or put any chapter title of this book in the blank space....

What is it about your relationships you need to understand?

What is it about your work that you need to understand, or sex, or being alone, or money, or creativity, or aging — or any other areas of your life you want to deal with?...

Simply ask a question, then sit in silence with it....

Ask a question, and then let all thought go....

Look at every answer that surfaces from within you....

Another way to phrase a good question is to ask something like, *"What is it about my* _____ *that is a teaching for me?"*

Or, *"How can I turn my* _____ *into my path to grace, ease, and lightness?"*

Or, *"What is it about my* _____ *that is teaching me to be free?"*

Simply ask a question, then let all thought go, and sit in silence with it....

Quietly, gently absorb the answers that come up for you.

You can do this practice any time and any place throughout your day. Ask yourself a question — *"What is it about my relationships I need to know to find a better way through life?"* — and then answer yourself with whatever words pop into your mind. Then ask again, if necessary, and answer again, until you feel satisfied with the answer.

This practice — simple though it is — can tune you into your intuitive teacher. It is almost always better to ask yourself questions rather than asking other people. Who knows you better than you?

Shattering Models

There is another simple concept that can help us make great leaps, quickly, in our lives once we understand it: the concept of *shattering models*. Every one of us has a set of models of the way things should be; we have created them for ourselves and accepted them from other people. They are mental and emotional models of how we should be and shouldn't be, what we should do and shouldn't do, and what we should have and shouldn't have. These models are deeply ingrained, from very early conditioning.

There comes a time when we become mature enough — in the highest sense of the word — to go beyond any and all of these models.

You can do, be, and have anything you wish,
in your heart.

Get married, or stay single...or get divorced. Have children, or don't have children. Love a woman, love a man. Love several women, love several men. Make a fortune, or make nothing. Be rich, be poor. Be a success, be a failure. Work for a corporation, work for yourself...or don't work at all. Be spiritual, or worldly...or political, or scientific...get into computers or covens, or both. You are free to do exactly as you wish — exactly as your heart desires — if you keep affirming it is so (and as long as it does no harm to others).

The only thing that blocks us from a life of freedom and wonder and light is our own model of what that freedom is, our own thoughts of what enlightenment should be. Once we simply let that model go — there's no way it *should* be, it is just what it is — we can accept what is, and finally be free to be ourselves, fully.

If we are truly free, we are free to do anything, to be anything, to have anything. So let all models go! Let a billion flowers bloom!

Quit judging yourself in any negative way. You are nothing less than a miracle of creation. When you realize that, you're free.

You're Free If You Affirm Yourself to Be

One of the deepest teachings we have seen repeatedly in this book is:

What you consistently affirm to yourself
soon becomes true in your experience.

Argue for your limitations, and they are yours. But affirm to yourself that you are free, creative, fulfilled — and soon you will find yourself creating a reality in which you're free, creative, fulfilled, in your own absolutely unique way.

You're free to do as you wish, to be what you wish, and to have what you wish. This is your birthright. You were meant to be as free as a bird, or a star, or any master who has walked this earth.

Embrace your freedom, your light, your love! It is yours for the taking.

Affirm it to be, and it will be. This is true. I know it in my heart, for I have seen it in my life.

May you be blessed with whatever your heart desires....
So be it — so it is!

16

Reflections

The following reflections are meant to be read at random. Give each one its own moment, for each in its own way can give you an experience of the powerful teachings of tantra.

Δ

Slow down as you read this.... Just take a few of these words, and sit with them, and quietly absorb them.

Give yourself the gift of silence, occasionally — even if it seems that nothing at all is happening. Rest assured that something *is* happening. Just let it happen, without expectations.

Just sit in silence once in a while, for a moment.... Within it are great treasures for you....

Δ

Sometimes you have to slow things down before you can see a whole new perspective on things — a broader perspective that opens up a world of possibilities.

Sometimes the best thing you can do is take a break....

Slow down....

Do nothing for a while.

And then you find you can see your ever-expanding, incredible life in a whole new way.

Δ

The little image between these reflections is a triangle pointing upward. It can be seen as a diagram of our path of consciousness.

You can look at human consciousness as a pyramid. Those at the bottom are consumed by fear. There is anxiety and violence. As we grow in the course of our lives, we move up the pyramid of consciousness, into the wonderful worlds where love overcomes fear.

And we open up our higher centers of consciousness: We open up our hearts, and ground our being in love....

And we open up our voices, and express our awareness to the world....

And we open up our third eye, our inner vision. And we come to see and understand the magical wonder of our creative minds....

And we connect with our crown chakra, and unite with the heavens, one with all....

Δ

This little image can also be looked at as a *stupa* — a pile of rocks, a pile of anything, shaped in a pyramid. In Tibet, there are piles of stones all over the place. I have two in my backyard: piles of extra bricks that I formed into a pyramid.

A stupa is a temple, in the best sense of the word — a place that connects you with spirit....

Use whatever image comes to mind, but find things in your life that remind you who you are, in reality: a spiritual being having a physical experience.

Δ

There's a great practice that can appeal to your lazy side: Just take some time to relax occasionally...now is a good time... just take a moment to relax as you read this, or hear this.... Go within while you relax....Connect with your presence, the wonder of who you are....Then dream on....

Dream of the life you want to live. If you dream it long enough, it will become reality.

Δ

The best teachers very rarely attempt to describe any kind of particular experience — the best teachers are the ones who show you how to open the doors into an infinite number of creative experiences within you....

The best teachers know and teach you to know *the truth is within you.*

Δ

So many people who become teachers or writers have had a legitimate, beautiful experience that they are trying to pass on to others. Yet so often their teachings, organizations, and systems become imbued with the idea that you have to do it *their way* — sometimes it's the way the original founder did it, other times it's the way that the tradition has developed over many years — when in fact there are an infinite number of ways to have a spiritual experience.

Tantra embraces everything, and so there are an infinite number of ways up the path. You're the only one who can walk your path, and your best guidance is found within.... Find your own guidance, find your own path, within your heart....

Δ

What is tantra?

It comes from the Sanskrit root word meaning "to *weave.*"

> **"Oh what a tangled web we weave**
> **when first we practice to deceive."**
> — Sir Walter Scott, *Marmion*

Here are some different ways to practice tantra:

Look at what you find yourself disliking.…
Look at your body aging.…
Look at old age.…
Look at sickness.…
Look at death.…
Look at insanity.…
Look at anything and everything you want to reject, and find
    a way to let it go.
Reject nothing.
Let everything go, and see the amazing perfection of it all.

Let the world become a beautiful place for you — in spite of so many apparent imperfections. Let go of how you think it *should* be…and see the beauty and perfection of *what is*…here and now, totally complete, totally perfect as it is.…

Every birth, every death, every accident, *everything* is completely as it should be — how could it be any other way?

Look at the perfection of our galaxies, our solar system, our earth, and our bodies.… We are perfect beings.

Let your true inner beauty shine forth. This is the highest teaching of tantra.

Δ

It just takes a single phrase or image to raise your consciousness into higher levels of awareness. Find a picture, or an object, or a written phrase — find something that reminds you of what you know — and carry it with you.

It can be a treasure map…a jewel…a ring…a picture of someone showering you with love from their eyes…a prayer, a song, a musical instrument…whatever resonates with you. And carry it with you, in your heart.

It is your reminder that all is perfect…there's nothing to worry about…the Universe provides for you…God is love.

Say it in whatever way you will.…

Δ

I must speak honestly some of my thoughts about many of the teachings, from East and West, that have become popular in America and other parts of the West today.

When I was studying Eastern practices and philosophies in my early and midtwenties, I went through a deep rejection of almost everything from my past, and from my culture and heritage in general.

One night, when I was deep into my studies of Tibetan Buddhism, I took a walk through the university campus in Berkeley, California. Then I strolled up Telegraph Avenue, then up the hill past the fraternities and sororities, toward the place I lived for over three years, the Tibetan Meditation Center.

As I approached the meditation center, wandering somewhat aimlessly, in no particular hurry to be anywhere, thinking many thoughts, a very clear voice suddenly spoke to me from within. It had a confident, forceful quality — something I've grown to understand and trust, for it was one of those moments when I connect with my intuitive teacher and the truth springs forth, loud and clear. The voice said,

> Look at yourself! Look at what you've been doing: When you went through the campus your mind was filled with thoughts of rejection, putting all the students down for their academic lives and for being constantly in their heads, their rational minds, and cutting off their emotions and their true experience.

> And when you went up Telegraph Avenue, you were rejecting the people on the street for being violent and stupid derelicts...and when you went by the fraternities, you were rejecting those people for being ignorant sheep, stupid macho drunkards...and when you went by the sororities, you rejected those women for being sheltered and sheepish and living in the past.

> Everyone you have encountered you have rejected! Is this what you want the result of your education to be?

And I realized that as long as I was rejecting so many things in life that I encountered along the way, I could not be free! True freedom certainly means being able to do anything, go any-where, with anyone, and find value and meaning in it, appreci-ating and enjoying what is.

That moment was a turning point for me. It forced me to take a good look at the attitudes that the teachings I was immersed in were fostering in me, and in others as well who were involved in similar kinds of study. I finally came to see that a lot of those teachings were creating as many neuroses as they were dissolv-ing. In rejecting so much of Western culture, I was rejecting my own roots. And when you reject your own roots, you cut yourself off from your intuition.

I finally had to leave the Tibetan Center and go elsewhere for teachings that would open me up to others rather than cut me off with a wall of rejection. I searched for, and found, teachings that were better adapted to the West. You can call it tantra for the West. You can call it the magical path. You can call it cre-ative visualization. You can call it spiritual soup. You can call it being sane. Call it what you will.

Δ

Living sanely and happily and comfortably is all just a matter of balance.

On the one hand, take the time and energy to dream, to imag-ine and to remember your dreams and desires as clearly and directly as possible...because you can have exactly what you want, if you visualize your wishes clearly and consistently, and take whatever obvious steps you need to take toward realizing those dreams....

On the other hand, learn to accept what is — whatever happens — with as few expectations as possible. Reject nothing. It's all happening for a very good reason, whether or not it's apparent to us at the time.

Δ

Here's a deep, ancient truth that every child knows. One very good practice is to sing this song, repeatedly, especially when you feel upset or distracted, and see that this song can be a powerful, life-changing mantra:

> **Row, row, row your boat**
> **Gently down the stream**
> **Merrily, merrily, merrily, merrily,**
> **Life is but a dream.**

Δ

Tibetan Buddhists — and many other wisdom teachers — say that reality can be perceived on three levels: outer, inner, and secret.

The outer plane is the physical plane — that which appears to the five outer senses — material, concrete reality.

The inner plane is the visionary plane within, perceived by the finer senses of our inner vision, our imagination, our intuition, our dreams. Some traditions call this the "astral plane," where magic occurs, the plane of mental creation that precedes physical creation.

The secret plane is even beyond this. It comprises the highest spiritual understanding of the wonder of what is…where we are all one, all part of one vast quantum field….

We are it…it is us…beyond words.

It is called secret not because anyone is trying to keep it a secret. It is "self-secret," because it must be grasped in a way that goes beyond our usual ways of learning and even perceiving.

A visionary is a person who sees on the inner and secret planes as well as on the outer plane….

Δ

The highest path of traditional Tantric Buddhism is called Dzog Chen, or "absolute perfection." For those who practice it, there are no special outer rituals, not necessarily even any inner practices. The only focus is on the innermost, the "secret": seeing the total perfection of what is, the perfection of every moment.

It takes a broad perspective to understand, but these words are true: Every moment of your life has been absolutely perfect. And it will continue to be so.

To quote a great teacher of Dzog Chen named Long Chen Pa, who lived seven hundred years ago:

> **Since everything is but an apparition,**
> **perfect in being what it is,**
> **having nothing to do with good or bad,**
> **acceptance or rejection,**
> **we may as well burst out in laughter.**
> — from *The Natural Freedom of Mind*

Δ

Here is a deep teaching of tantra — and of a great many other traditions as well.

We are multidimensional beings. We have different levels of being, which can be called "bodies." We function on four different levels, simultaneously: We can call them the physical, the emotional, the mental, and the spiritual. We have a physical body, emotions, thoughts, and a spirit. As we move from the physical to the spiritual, each level of being, each body, becomes finer and larger, encompassing more space and awareness.

Some people focus almost entirely on their physical level of being. Their awareness is centered on their body, or others' bodies — their strength, their weakness, their aches and pains, their needs, their health, the perfect diet, the latest techniques for healthful living, their looks, their lover's looks, their attractiveness or unattractiveness, their tensions, their digestion, their operations, and on and on. They eat too much, or they don't eat enough, with a neurotic need to be skinny and fashionable.

I don't mean to reject the physical plane in any way — it is beautiful, it is a key to the infinite…it is pleasurable, it is perfect. But focusing *solely* on the physical plane — or any other plane, for that matter — is excessive and leads to a narrow, limited view of reality.

Some people focus almost exclusively on their emotional level of being. They are deeply involved in their personal dramas, their highs and their lows. They are overwhelmed by the waves of their emotions; their feelings have complete control over their behavior. Their continual focus is on their feelings, or on others' feelings — whether they're comfortable, or upset, or feeling fearful or guilty, or feeling high and clear.

They may drink too much, or take any number of drugs to alter their feelings or even obliterate them so they don't have to deal with them. Or they may be excessively moderate and rigid, not allowing themselves to do a great number of spontaneous things. They may have deeply repressed feelings of anger or hostility that they would never allow themselves to express, so they create a tension in their body that drives them to escapism and excess in many forms, such as food, drugs, alcohol, and even a wide variety of physical and emotional diseases.

This is not to reject the emotional plane in any way (or drugs or alcohol or food either — for they can all be used skillfully and pleasurably). Our emotions are wonderful — they are perfect;

they are a key to the infinite. Our emotions are the key to our intuition, to our inner guidance and our psychic senses. But focusing entirely on the emotional plane is excessive, and leads to a narrow, limited view of our lives and our possibilities.

Some people focus primarily on their mental level of being. The ideas of their minds are the only things worthwhile. Many of these people are in the universities and in the sciences. Their continual focus is on their own or others' brilliant scholarship or ideas; they mostly talk about recent books, or someone's theories, or perhaps someone's neuroses or stupidity or brilliance. They may be completely out of touch with their physical or emotional or spiritual bodies, lost in their mental life. They may feel that the scientific method — which they define as being a purely rational device — is the only valid basis for any belief, and they may thoroughly reject anything that has to do with the intuitive or psychic (and comes through emotional and spiritual bodies) such as spiritual healing or psychic awareness or creative visualization or true magic.

This is not to reject the mental plane in any way: It is a fantastically powerful, essential tool…it is perfect. But focusing purely on the mental plane ignores too many other phases of our existence. Einstein put it brilliantly:

The intuitive mind is a sacred gift
and the rational mind is a faithful servant.
We have created a society that honors the servant
and has forgotten the gift.

There are also people who focus purely on the spiritual level of being. Their continual focus is on their spiritual development, or the level of achievement of their teachers or gurus, or the level of their friends' or other people's spiritual awareness. Many of them reject physical, emotional, and sometimes even mental ways of being altogether, in themselves and in others.

Every level of being has its own truth and perfection and power …yet every level has its own neuroses, if they aren't balanced with an awareness of the other levels. For every level of the divine Tree of Life — the structure of the universe in the words of the Kabbala — is connected to every other level. It is all one. We are physical, emotional, mental, and spiritual beings. We are all of it.

Embrace all of yourself, without rejecting any part. Don't reject anything about your body, your emotions, your mind, or your spirit. They are phenomenal things. They are perfect.

Δ

Look at the Tarot card of the magician — and see that it is you....

Everyone is a magician, a creator…channeling the energy of the Universe into the creation of whatever she or he chooses.

We have within us the magical implements to create whatever we wish: the wand of the creative mind, the sword of our personal power, the cup of inspiration, and the pentacle of abundance and magical creation.

All these tools are within us, waiting to be used....All the higher forces of the universe are at hand, waiting to be called.

THE MAGICIAN.

**Ask and you shall receive, seek and you will find.
Knock and the door will be opened unto you....**

Δ

A deep teaching:

Realize your own power. Grasp your worth, your wonderful creativity on your unique path....Your power and creativity are readily available in your dreams, your inner vision, your insight....Realize that you have the ability to manifest the life of your dreams....

Most of us, for a great many reasons, gave away the natural power and vision we had as children. First we gave it away to our parents, then we gave it away to our friends. And what they thought and felt became very important to us. We gave it to our teachers and felt we knew nothing.

Now is the time to take it back. Trust yourself. Trust your feelings, always. You are a powerful being; once you realize that, your path becomes clear.

All great philosophies, all great spiritual paths, encourage us to do the same thing:

Know thyself.

Who are you? That's a great question to ask, and ponder.

Who are you? You are far more than a physical body — you are a physical, mental, emotional, and spiritual being.

Your physical body will pass away. Your thoughts and feelings come and go. Your spirit — your spiritual being — never changes, never dies.

You are that.

You are one with spirit. You are one with the creative energy of the universe. That is who you are.

Δ

Let us take a journey now, you and I....

Together we can travel a great distance — much farther than mere miles on this planet, much farther than the stars....For this journey is within the realm of the mind....And this realm of our mind encompasses all of space, all of the universe....

And every imagined limitation of time and space dissolves as we open the doors to this realm of the mind.

How do we open these doors?

Simply relax...trust yourself....

Relax, take a few deep breaths, and let yourself sink deep within....

Relax, and let yourself be....

Let yourself drift into an infinite awareness that encompasses everything....

Become aware of the field of light that endlessly showers you with the energy of the universe, the blessings of life....

It is an infinite awareness that you can direct anywhere you wish in your creative imagination....

You take it from here....

**You can create
whatever your heart desires!
So be it. So it is.**

Δ

Addendum

Tantra in the East
A Brief History of Tibetan Tantric Buddhism

Tibetan Buddhism is often called the tantric branch of Buddhism. Here's a brief overview of it, gleaned from several years of study. It's not a scholarly approach — that's already been well represented by numerous writers and teachers. This is, instead, a compilation of writings and stories that I picked up from books and from the Tibetan people themselves, presented in an informal fashion — in the spirit in which I heard most of these stories.

I heard many of these things when I studied the Nyingma tradition of Tibetan Buddhism (the oldest of the four schools of Tibetan Buddhism), so if it seems to glorify that school and slightly minimize the others, you'll know why. We'll end by looking at what really matters in all these stories, their meaning and usefulness in the world today.

The Historical Roots of Tantra

There are two main streams of tantra in our heritage, usually called Buddhist tantra and Hindu tantra. Most of my education was in Buddhist tantra, which is more recent than Hindu tantra.

Hindu tantra includes the followers of Shiva, the Cosmic Dancer. He dances on our bodies, a symbol of destruction. The Hindu trinity is Brahma, the Creator; Vishnu, the Sustainer; and Shiva, the Destroyer, and all have their perfect place and time. Hindu tantra is a beautiful tradition — but here I'll concentrate on Buddhist tantra, which flourished in Tibet until 1959, when China moved in and violently took control and did their best to drive Buddhism out of the country, fulfilling an ancient prophecy.

Most Tibetans are staunch Buddhists, and their history really begins with the advent of Buddhism in their country. Today Tibetans often say that before Buddhism, they were a wild people, "blue-faced monkeys," after the practice they had of painting their faces blue when waging war. They were known as fierce warriors, and they practiced a form of magic that was very powerful — and sometimes very destructive — known as Bon (pronounced *bone*) magic.

By 800 CE Buddhism had been flourishing and spreading for 1,300 years — the Buddha, Shakyamuni Gautama, taught in India in 500 BCE. In those 1,300 years, Buddhism spread south and east, to Sri Lanka, Burma, Thailand, Vietnam, Cambodia, Laos, and Malaysia; it spread north to China and Mongolia; and it spread into Japan, where it evolved into Zen. Buddhism covered much of the East, most of Asia, and had a great impact on all the countries that adopted it.

But it was unable to penetrate Tibet, mainly because of the powerful opposition of the Bon religion, and because of the people's inability to understand the principles of the so-called religion, or philosophy, or set of teachings leading to liberation that is known as Buddhism.

The king of Tibet in the eighth century is one of the most famous and revered in Tibetan history, because he was the one who initiated the founding of the new religion, the new teachings that transformed the lives of all the people in the country. He was named Trisong Detsen, and it is said he was an incarnated king — in a previous lifetime, he had created enough good karma to be reborn not only as a king but as someone who was open and ready for the truth of the dharma, the universal teachings of the Buddha.

The king became a student of Buddhism, and his understanding grew rapidly. He tried many times to introduce the great teachings into his country, and brought in several well-known and powerful people from India to do it, including the great saint Shanti Rakshita, but they were all unable to do it. Every time they attempted to build a temple, it would be destroyed through the efforts of the Bon magicians. There were earthquakes, and lightning strikes, and anything the Buddhists attempted to build was quickly destroyed.

Finally, the king summoned the great magician, mystic, and teacher named Padma Sambhava to come to Tibet. Padma Sambhava was born in an ancient land called Urgyan or Uddiyana, which is probably part of present-day Nepal. Many legends surround the life and teachings of Padma Sambhava. His name literally means "Lotus Born," because he is said to have been discovered as a one-year-old child, sitting in the center of a huge lotus flower in the middle of a sacred lake named Dhanakosha. He was deep in meditation, with sweat on his brow.

He was found by a princess and taken to the palace and brought up to be a king. But he tired of the royal life, and went off in search of the deepest and most profound teachings he could find. It is said that Padma Sambhava studied with Ananda, the Buddha's favorite disciple, a man with a huge, open heart and a phenomenal memory who memorized all of the Buddha's 84,000 oral teachings or *sutras*. If so, that would make Padma Sambhava 1,300 years old, at least by Western calculating, by the time he came to Tibet. It is said that Padma Sambhava had mastered a great many powers, one of which was the power of a very long life.

After studying with Ananda and other great teachers of Buddhism at the time in India, Padma Sambhava had many adventures; he wandered through India for many years, and spent five years meditating in each of the eight great cemeteries of India. He built houses of bones and lived in them, a freak and a recluse. And in those cemeteries he was given the great teachings of tantra by *dakinis* — women of many different forms, some spiritual and angelic, some physical and human — who came to him in meditation. He became an adept, then a great master, and his fame spread wide.

The king of Tibet invited him to come to his country and establish the dharma. Padma Sambhava came, and the king met him at the border of Tibet. The king, of course, assumed that this teacher would bow down before him, as everyone else did. But Padma Sambhava did not bow down before the king. The king was perplexed, but the histories say that Padma Sambhava simply raised one finger, and a lightning bolt shot from the tip of it and stopped a very short distance from the king's nose. The king, in awe, fell on his knees in supplication and became one of Padma Sambhava's most powerful disciples and allies.

The histories of Tibet are colorful, unusual, and amazing. They are unlike the histories of the West in many ways — unless you count the Bible as a historical work. For like the Bible, Tibetan histories are filled with tales that many people reject as impossible and untrue. You can accept or reject these stories as you will; it doesn't matter. For my part, I think they are wonderful, in the deepest sense of the word — filled with wonder and light and deep teachings for us, if we have ears to hear.

Many people tend to be skeptical about the miracles that are part of other people's traditions, yet many of these same people believe in the miracles of Christ, the Genesis stories of creation and the great flood, Moses turning a stick into a snake and crossing the Red Sea, and so on. So often we accept the familiar and reject the unfamiliar. But back to our story…

Padma Sambhava went into Tibet and made plans to build the first Buddhist temple at a place called Kagyu Samye Ling. He told the king that, in order to build it, he had to first be able to meditate in absolute uninterrupted silence, and he went up into an isolated cave.

After a while, a most remarkable man came to the king — he was well dressed, very striking — and told the king that he was vastly wealthy and had a great gift for the king to support him in his efforts to build a temple: He would deliver all the red cedar the king needed. Cedar in Tibet is a very rare and precious commodity, because it has to be hauled in through hundreds of rough, mountainous miles. The king was overwhelmed at the man's offer, and the man said that the king should tell Padma Sambhava about it immediately.

The king replied that Padma Sambhava was in meditation and did not want to be disturbed. The man said that he was certain that if Padma Sambhava knew of this gift, he would want to be told about it. He would want his meditation interrupted, because he has fulfilled the goal of his meditation.

So the king went up to the cave and entered. In the depths of the cave it is told that he saw, at first, not Padma Sambhava in meditation but a *garuda* bird — a huge bird with strong arms as well as wings, a symbol of power and spiritual flight. The *garuda* was devouring a large *naga*, or snake — a symbol of the dark forces that were preventing the Tibetans from reaching their goals. The *garuda* had almost entirely devoured the snake — only the tail was left, dangling from its beak. As soon as the great bird saw the king, his eyes grew large, and a fierce struggle ensued. The snake gained strength and was able to release itself from the *garuda*'s massive jaws and get out of the cave with astounding speed. The king could do nothing — even as the snake whipped right past him.

The *garuda* instantly transformed back into Padma Sambhava — and he was enraged at the king. He shouted, "Why did you interrupt me?" And the king said he had been told to talk to him, because a fantastic man had given them all the cedarwood they needed to build their temple.

Padma Sambhava shouted, "You fool! That was the king of the *nagas*, getting you to break my meditation. Because of it, he's gotten away, and out of my control!" The king felt crushed, and he must have felt very strange when Padma Sambhava continued with these words — words that have been famous throughout the history of Tibet:

"In spite of your interruption, I will be able to establish Buddhism in this country. And it will be embraced by the people, and will blossom and flower. But, because of your interruption, this is what I see:

**"When iron birds fly,
and people travel in machines without horses,
Buddhism will be driven from this country
by armies from the north.
The great teachings will be crushed in Tibet,
and will move to the West,
to the land of the red man."**

The king could make little sense of these predictions, for they weren't to come true for another 1,150 years or so. Saddened and disheartened, he returned home. Padma Sambhava returned to his meditation, and soon they were able to construct a great temple at Kagyu Samye Ling and the powerful teachings of Buddhism were introduced to the Tibetan people. The king became one of Padma Sambhava's most evolved disciples. Twenty-five other disciples became very famous, as well. A Tibetan woman named Yeshe Tsogyal became known as Padma Sambhava's chief *dakini* and disciple and biographer, and it is said that she was able to understand and transmit all his teachings and all his awareness — something no other disciple accomplished.

The story of Buddhism in Tibet is really the story of Padma Sambhava, because he is the great founder and fountainhead of it all, and he is revered by the Tibetan people much as Christ is revered in the West. He is called the father of Buddhist tantra — and his brilliant contribution to Tibet, and now to the whole world, is his adaptation of the teachings of the Buddha into a form that people can readily understand and apply in their daily lives.

The original spoken words of Buddha in India, called the sutras, are the work of a mind of phenomenal intellect and power and breadth and depth. His original words were presented to a people who were highly civilized, highly evolved, and intelligent. The people of Tibet, however, were wild, relatively uneducated, emotional, intense, and not at all suited to hear teachings that were so subtle, sublime, and intellectually demanding.

And so the teachings needed to be adapted to the people of Tibet. Padma Sambhava was able to translate Buddha's teachings so that the people could grasp them thoroughly. He did this by writing and introducing and practicing the *tantras*. He adapted the sutras of the Buddha into tantras — written and spoken teachings that were highly pragmatic, physical, and comparatively nonintellectual. The teachings were adapted to meet the needs of the people, just as they're being adapted into the West today, to meet the needs of a very different people, with a very different mentality and culture.

Padma Sambhava's main disciples became known as the "twenty-five great siddhas," because each of them is said to have attained a great power, or *siddhi*. With the assistance of these disciples, Padma Sambhava was able to firmly establish the liberating teachings of Buddhism in Tibet, in spite of a great deal of powerful opposition. The teachings swept across the entire country and had a transformative impact on the people and their way of life; the country was changed from bottom to top, from the lives of the simplest common people to the entire political structure, through the introduction of a set of teachings now known as Buddhist tantra.

The Nyingma School

Padma Sambhava and his disciples established what later came to be called the Nyingma tradition. *Nyingma* means "ancient ones" or "the old school" — it was called that only later, of course, after the new schools developed. For several hundred years, there was basically one school of Buddhism in Tibet. And then, as in all human movements, like Christianity in the West, other branches formed when strong leaders came along and adapted or changed the teachings, or generated new teachings based on their own experience.

The Nyingma, the first school in Tibet, was criticized by those in newly developing schools because they felt that the Nyingma school was too similar to the original Bon magic. The teachings of Buddha originally had to adapt a great deal to penetrate into the country. Once they were successfully adapted, they laid the foundations for other schools to come along and claim that they had adapted too much, that they were too much like their wild, magical predecessors.

It was a natural inclination, a natural cycle. Some people who had been born and raised in the Buddhist tradition even claimed that Nyingma was just the Bon ritual in reverse — that their altars and practices were very similar, except that they mirrored and reversed each other. The Nyingmas always spun their prayer wheels and did their circumambulations (walking in a circle, chanting or meditating) in a clockwise direction, for example, while the Bon magicians spun their prayer wheels and did their circumambulations in a counterclockwise direction. In the Nyingma tradition, deities are placed on the altar in a certain arrangement; in the Bon tradition, the placement is similar but reversed.

The Nyingmas, of course, did not agree with their critics and did not change their ways. The tradition continues today as one of the most vital of all the schools of Tibetan Buddhism.

The Gelugpa School

The newer, so-called reformed schools, in reaction to a tradition they felt was too close to the Bon school, claimed they were getting back closer to the original purity of Buddhism in India. One of the most notable of the reformed schools was the Gelugpa, which sprang from the teachings of a man named Tsongkhapa, who lived in the thirteenth century, several hundred years after the Nyingma school was established.

The Gelugpas became popular and powerful and ended up gaining most of the political control of the country by about 1800 CE. Tibet's system of government was unusual, nearly unique in world history: The spiritual leaders were also the political leaders. The head of the Gelugpa sect is the Dalai Lama, and he, during the course of several hundred years and over two dozen incarnations, became the political leader of much of Tibet. (Those from eastern Tibet, like my Nyingma teacher, claimed that they were virtually independent from Gelugpa rule.)

The Gelugpas developed a highly scholarly tradition, very much in contrast to the Nyingmas' more pragmatic and practical approach to Buddha's teachings.

The Kagyud School

Another school that developed later was called the Kagyud school. The Kagyud is similar in many ways to the Nyingma school, stressing practice and personal experience rather than intellectual knowledge. The tradition of the Kagyuds came through a different source than the Nyingma. It's an important tradition, still being carried on in India and in the West today. The Nyingma tradition, as we have seen, stems primarily from the teachings of Padma Sambhava and claims to go directly back to Shakyamuni Buddha. The Kagyud tradition stems from an original and powerful teacher named Tilopa, whose life illustrates the essence of tantra.

It all began back in India, probably around 800 CE. By this time Buddhism had spread throughout India, and the Mahayana — the outreaching form of Buddhism, the Buddhism of the *bodhisattva*, dedicated to helping all beings attain enlightenment — was in full flower. There were many great Buddhist universities throughout India, the greatest of which was Nalanda University. The most well-known, well-educated, and powerful teacher at Nalanda was named Naropa. He had thousands of disciples and was revered as a great Mahayana Buddhist, a great scholar and teacher.

The histories say that one night Naropa had a dream, and in the dream, a wild, naked old *dakini* (a woman who brings teachings) came to him, dancing furiously, laughing at him, pointing, shrieking, saying, "You think you are such a great scholar! If you really want to know the teachings, listen to the first name that you hear tomorrow, and find him and learn his teachings. If you don't do this, you will never really understand the truth! You are stuck in your own pride!" And she laughed at him wildly.

He woke up in a cold sweat, deeply unsettled by his vivid dream. He walked over to his window, and beneath his balcony he heard three beggars talking, and they mentioned a great yogi named Tilopa. As soon as he heard the name, a deep knowing flashed through his whole being — he knew he must find the great yogi Tilopa, whoever he was, because he had deep teachings for him, far beyond anything he had ever encountered before. Naropa, a patriarch for thousands, became like a little child that day.

That same day he informed his disciples he was leaving to go in search of his new teacher. His disciples were deeply upset, and begged and pleaded with him to stay and teach, for he was their greatest teacher — how could he leave them when they needed his guidance and light? But he said that he had to go and that they would find their own way. And then he wandered off, in search of Tilopa.

He covered the entire vast country, asking everywhere for the great yogi Tilopa. But no one had ever heard of him. He refused to get discouraged and began asking at the smallest towns and tiniest villages, wandering, canvassing the entire country again, asking everyone he encountered.

Ten years passed — ten years of fruitless wandering. And yet he was undaunted. Twelve years passed, and yet he persisted, and kept looking for a man no one had ever heard of. Finally, at the beginning of his thirteenth year of wandering, at a very small village on the southern coast of India, as he asked for the great yogi Tilopa, some people laughed and said, "We don't know any great yogi Tilopa, but there's a bum named Tilopa who lives down at the beach. He's so lazy, he doesn't do anything but lie around all day. He doesn't work. All he eats are the fish heads the fishermen throw away."

Naropa went in search of him, and found an old, grizzled bum lying on the sand, doing nothing. He asked if his name was Tilopa. The man nodded. He asked for his instruction. The man laughed, and kept lying there, half asleep, totally ignoring Naropa. Naropa asked again for his instruction, and got absolutely no response.

For three days, Tilopa just lay there, doing nothing, eating some fish heads now and then, completely ignoring Naropa, acting as if he was not there at all. Finally, at the end of the third day, he turned to Naropa and nodded, saying without a word that he would take him as a disciple, if he was strong enough and open enough to receive his teachings. Over the course of the following years, the great Naropa was slowly whittled down, and the highly esteemed and respected scholar and teacher became a bum just like Tilopa.

For years Tilopa gave Naropa no teachings, but just kept ordering him to do things that got him in trouble or caused him great pain. One day, for example, he told Naropa of a wedding feast that was happening nearby, and he asked him to crash the feast and bring him something for his dinner. This was considered extremely rude and unacceptable in India, but nevertheless, Naropa went to the wedding, pretended to be a guest, and got himself a dinner that he brought back to Tilopa, who devoured every bit of it, quickly and greedily. Then he told Naropa to go back and get himself a supper — so Naropa went back once again, but this time he was discovered, thrown out of the party, severely beaten, and tossed into a ditch. Tilopa found him there, bleeding and bruised and dazed, and he laughed and laughed and went on his way, leaving Naropa to nurse his wounds.

Another time they were wandering through the jungle and came to a little stream, about five feet across. Tilopa told Naropa to lie down across the stream so that he could cross over on Naropa's back. Naropa obeyed and Tilopa walked on his back, and when Naropa got up he found his body was covered with huge leeches, for the stream was infested with them. Again, Tilopa laughed and laughed as Naropa frantically tore the leeches from his body.

Twelve years went by. Naropa stayed with Tilopa all that time, and no teachings were given — at least nothing that had the appearance of a teaching. It was simply a matter of living from day to day.

The histories become even more incredible at this point — more mystical, more miraculous, much like the story of Christ walking on water or healing Lazarus. At one point Tilopa and Naropa were walking along and came to a high cliff with jagged rocks several hundred feet below. Tilopa said, "If you have faith in me as your teacher, dive off that cliff!" Naropa took one look at the rocks below... and dove. His body smashed into the rocks and he was killed instantly.

Then Tilopa began demonstrating some of his powers. He sat cross-legged at the top of the cliff and did a powerful chant that healed Naropa's broken bones and torn and bleeding skin. Naropa gained consciousness, and was alive and well.

One day Tilopa stared at Naropa, motionless, for a long time. Naropa was now a very different person than the one who came to him twelve years before — his pride was gone, his arrogance was gone, his role-playing as a scholar and teacher was gone. He was open, like a child.

Tilopa took off his beat-up sandal and without a word of warning smashed Naropa in the face with it. Naropa's mind went into a kind of shock — and the aftermath of that shock propelled him into a great space, a light he'd never imagined, never known or experienced before.

Tilopa said, "Now you are ready — ready for the great teachings of the Mahamudra." And Tilopa passed on all the teachings of the lineage to Naropa — teachings he had received from teachers beyond the physical plane, in direct spiritual transmission. For it is taught that Tilopa got his teachings from celestial sources, from no one incarnated in a physical body, but rather from the great teachers of Buddha and Christ and everyone else who has deep understanding gained from sources other than teachers who walk this earth.

And so Naropa received the great teachings of the Mahamudra, which literally means "the great gesture." It embodies a large number of teachings that have been recorded and translated today, and serves as a cornerstone of much of Buddhist tantra.

Naropa's greatest disciple was a Tibetan named Marpa, who made the perilous journey from Tibet to India three times, bringing great offerings of gold. Naropa passed on the teachings of the Mahamudra to Marpa, who became known as the Translator, for he translated the teachings of India into Tibetan.

Marpa the Translator's greatest disciple was a skinny little yogi named Milarepa, who became famous for his songs and his divine ecstatic vision as well as for his simple, austere life and his great yogic power. Through the lineage of Tilopa, Naropa, Marpa, and Milarepa came the great school of the Kagyud. It is very close to the Nyingma in many ways, and many of the great teachers throughout Tibetan history studied with both schools.

Today, eight branches of the Kagyud exist. One of the most important of these branches is the Karma Kagyud, which is led by the famous Karmapa, who is a seer, a visionary leader respected and consulted by all the schools.

The Sakya School

Four great schools developed in Tibet, and grew strong and prospered, until well into the middle of the twentieth century. The other prominent school that developed is the Sakya school. Its traditions are also very similar to those of the Nyingma school. Originally, most Nyingmas were located east of Lhasa, while the Sakyas were based west of Lhasa. Most were farmers; many lived close to the Nepal border and were able to escape the Chinese invasion. They now align themselves with the Nyingma and Kagyud.

The Rivalry

There was, and still is, rivalry among the different schools, but many students and most of the great teachers, the great *lamas*, have studied in several schools and taught students of different schools. The branches are not nearly so separate as Christian churches tend to be.

And in many ways these traditions aren't as *serious* as many branches of religion in the West are. As Tibetan Buddhism grew to embrace the whole culture, it reflected the joy and spontaneity and freedom of a truly unique people. When I was studying with Lama Tarthang Tulku, in Berkeley, California, we would often try, especially in our intense and demanding language classes, to get him off the subject he was trying to teach and into the many stories of his childhood in Tibet, which were fascinating. Perhaps this one story will give you a better glimpse of Tibetan history than you could get from a great many books.

There are a whole series of stories and jokes about a wandering Nyingma yogi in ancient Tibet. Many of the stories are very much like our traveling salesman jokes — only they're "wandering yogi" jokes. Some of them are explicitly, uninhibitedly sexual. Here's one that's a bit different.

Once upon a time, many years ago, there was a terrible drought in parts of Tibet. Crops were drying up, animals were suffering. A thousand Gelugpa monks gathered on the floor of a great valley and chanted for rain. They chanted for ten days and ten nights — and yet the skies remained deep and blue and dry.

Then a wandering Nyingma yogi came up to the monks. He looked at them and laughed. He was wearing a tattered robe (a *chuba*), tied at the waist. He climbed a tree right in front of them and hung on a branch by his knees, upside down. His robe fell over his head, exposing his bare ass hanging in the tree. He let loose a loud fart that resounded through the valley…and suddenly the sky filled with huge, billowing rain clouds, and they were all drenched in rain.

He ran away, laughing, yelling out to them, "See! One Nyingma fart is worth ten thousand Gelugpa chants!"

This history is brief and unscholarly. There is much more that could be said. But history is important only in the ways that it reflects our lives today, and affects us here and now. So we'll move on....

Tibetan Buddhism Today

In 1959 Padma Sambhava's predictions came true. The government to the north of Tibet, isolated from them by the great wall of the Himalayan Mountains, had been very aggressive for thousands of years. In 1959 armies marched in from the north and forcefully took over Tibet — an imperialistic move that will have negative karmic results for China, just as the United States and Russia have been faced with the negative karmic consequences of their imperialism. For you simply can't move into another country and take it over by force without suffering deep karmic results that will someday balance the scales of justice. As you sow, so you shall reap.

China took over Tibet and forcefully drove out Buddhism. This domination and exploitation have resulted in a worldwide pro-Tibet movement; the story of Buddhism in Tibet is not over. (If China were smart, it would realize that if Buddhism were restored in Tibet, it would become a spiritual tourist attraction that would rival any other tourist attraction in the world.)

In one way these very unfortunate circumstances for Tibet were fortunate for the West, because they forced many lamas, including the Dalai Lama, Chögyam Trungpa, Tarthang Tulku, the Karmapa, and many others (representing all four schools), out of Tibet. And their teachings are being adapted to a strange new land we call the West.

America, compared to Tibet, is extremely violent and igno-rant — unaware of the law of karma, unaware of the means of attaining true freedom and fulfillment. But America's vision-ary constitutional policy of freedom of religion makes it one of the most fertile and open countries on earth. And so it is in America and Europe that the ancient teachings of Tibetan tantra are blossoming, in many new forms — some very tra-ditional, some completely transformed into the new cultural context. Western tantra is being born as Buddhist tantra is driven from its homeland.

What exactly do we mean when we say *Buddhist tantra*? The tantra is a vast body of written and spoken teachings, a great many of which spring either directly or indirectly from Padma Sambhava. They teach that there are nine levels of Buddhism, nine levels of the teachings of the dharma, which can be simply translated as "the truth." The first level is called the *hinayana* (or the Theravadan school), the so-called smaller vehicle. This is the teaching that the Tibetan sources, at least, say is self-centered, because it is focused simply on the personal salvation of the aspirant. (Those who embrace Theravadan Buddhism will of course completely disagree with this.)

The next two of the nine stages are the *mahayana*, or the "great vehicle," which is focused on the transformation and enlightenment of all humankind, and of every animal and plant on the planet. The Mahayana is the path of the bodhisattva, who takes a vow not to attain final enlightenment until every animal and plant and person on the planet has attained enlightenment.

The six paths beyond the Mahayana are called the *vajrayana*, or "diamond vehicle," or Buddhist tantra. The six levels evolve first in outer, then inner, then secret stages. The first two levels, the first practices, are the outer Vajrayana — involving practices that are done on outer, obvious levels that other people can easily see. Those who practice on these levels often wear robes, and there is public knowledge of the practices.

The inner level, however — the next two stages of the Vajrayana — gives us a set of higher teachings and finer practices that are not necessarily reflected on the outer level. The practices are done in an internal way, and anyone can do them, without having to adapt a certain lifestyle.

Then the deepest levels, the secret levels, unfold — the highest levels of the Vajrayana. Here the practices take place on a deep, subtle level that goes beyond the inner level. When they use the term *secret* Tibetan teachers often say that they are not intentionally trying to keep secrets from anyone but that the contents of the teachings by their very nature are "self-secret" — they simply cannot be communicated in spoken or written words... they cannot be taught, they must be caught, directly, intuitively.

The highest level of Buddhist tantra, the ninth level, is called Dzog Chen, or the level of "absolute perfection." This is the highest level of awareness possible, which sees the total perfection in every level of the teachings, and in every level of our understanding, from ignorance to enlightenment. This is the path that embraces *all* the teachings, all the ways of life, and sees that every one of us has our own path, our own understanding and karma, and that it is perfect for every one of us to be exactly where we are.

The highest level of Buddhist tantra embraces every path, including *hinayana*, because it embraces everything and everyone, and every way of life. The greatest teaching of Buddhist tantra is the perfection of all paths. It is perfect for you to be doing exactly what you are doing at this moment. When you realize this, you are free.

Tantra in the West

Tantra is vital to the West today, because of its capacity for infinite adaptability in the creative hands and minds of its practitioners. The teachings of Buddha — outer, inner, and secret — went through a complete metamorphosis in the hands of Padma Sambhava, so that he could present them in a form that the wild, warlike Tibetans could understand. Once again, the great teachings are being adapted to a wild and warlike culture we call the modern world.

Though the forms are changing completely, the essence of the teachings — the shimmering, wonderful essence of all spiritual truths of all cultures — remains the same. And by discovering the truths at the core of our life, the root of our being, we become free, free to fully be ourselves, free to dream, free to create.

By living these teachings, we can change our community, our nation, our world into a place that respects all human life — and *all* life — and that will never again fight violent and destructive wars in order to try to achieve political and material things that we don't even need for our happiness or freedom.

The teachings of tantra have spread around the world. And they show us that we have always had the teachings, the answers, the way to complete freedom deep within our own hearts, and deep within our cultural heritage.

We'll close by pondering once again one of those teachings. Understanding it in our experience, in the depths of our being, completely transforms us. We have heard these words before — and, if we can grasp them, nothing more need be understood:

**Everything has an outer, inner,
and secret level of existence.**

That includes you. Your outer level of being is obvious and apparent to one and all. Your inner level of being, filled with its streams of thought and waves of emotion, is known and felt only by you.

Your secret level of being is something to ponder and meditate on, something to discover and have revealed to you in all its shining glory:

You are light,
pure and free and eternal.

You are enlightened. You always have been. Once this is revealed and understood, you are free, loving, endlessly creative.

This is who you are, on your deepest, most expansive level of being: You are pure light, life, and love, unrestrained, unbound, and infinite.

You are one with all creation.

You are that.
That is all there is.

Honor it. Realize it, now. Live it, every moment.

This great teaching is beautifully expressed in the words of someone from another tradition that has also spread around the world:

The kingdom of heaven
is within.

So be it. So it is!

Acknowledgments and Notes

First of all, I have to thank my beautiful wife, Auri, for supporting my dreams so passionately, and for giving me the time and space when I need it. And thanks to Kai, for being who you are, and bringing endless awe and wonder into my life.

Thanks to everyone at New World Library and Publishers Group West — you've helped me fulfill my dream.

1 The Direct Path of Tantra

— The story "Three Different Paths" was told to me by Lama Tarthang Tulku, in Berkeley, California.

— Many of the ideas and practices in the section called "Confronting Negative Feelings" are from Shakti Gawain, author of *Creative Visualization*. This area is a specialty of hers. The technique of shouting in the car when driving alone to release anger was suggested by Pamela Whitney. Yelling at a pillow is a well-known Gestalt technique.

— The four-step process in "A Tantric Practice" was taught to me by Shakti Gawain, who was given it in a workshop led by Edward O'Hara in Marin County, California.

2 The Power of Affirmations

— I first learned about affirmations from Catherine Ponder, author and Unity Church minister. I have to thank her for the words that have changed my life: *"In an easy and relaxed manner, a healthy and positive way, in its own perfect time, for the highest good of all...."*

— Many of the ideas in "The Act of Creation" section are from Israel Regardie, author of *The Art of True Healing, The Tree of Life*, and many other books.

— Many of the ideas in the "Writing Affirmations" section came from Shakti Gawain, who got them from Sondra Ray and others. Sondra Ray's book *I Deserve Love* describes the technique. Shakti Gawain's book *Creative Visualization* is an excellent source for affirmations and many other techniques. It was from a minister named Marc Reymont and then later from various recovery programs that I heard the somewhat startling statement that you should be able to achieve results with any affirmation within twenty-one days.

3 Relationships

— I want to acknowledge Shakti Gawain's clarity and vision in the arena of relationships. Her book *The Relationship Handbook* is wonderful and powerful.

— Shakti Gawain's mother, Elizabeth Gawain, contributed the second paragraph in the "What Do You Want?" section.

— The late Shirley Luthman gave us the four possible reactions to feedback in the section called "The Outer World."

6 Work

— "Your Ideal Scene," as well as a great many other practices in this book, were things Shakti Gawain and I both did in our workshops for many years.

7 Money

— The "Creative Meditation for Money" is my own free adaptation of Israel Regardie's meditations in his excellent book *The Art of True Healing*.

8 Creativity

— Ken Keyes Jr., author of *Handbook to Higher Consciousness*, told me the story of being tucked into bed at night in the "Dealing with Your Inner Critic" section.

9 Food and Drink

— The translation of the verse from *Shodoka* was given to me by Robert Aitkin at the Maui Zendo, Maui, Hawaii. It is reprinted here with his kind permission.

10 Meditation and Yoga

— In the section titled "Silence," the Tibetan approach came from Lama Tarthang Tulku, in Berkeley, California. The traditional Buddhist meditation was given to me by Elizabeth Gawain.

— I found the technique of grounding, described in the "Pillar of Light" section, at the Berkeley Psychic Institute through a teacher named David Lovegarden. I learned the technique of sending a healing from Mildred Jackson, author of *The Handbook of Alternatives to Chemical Medicine* and the greatest healer I have ever been blessed to know.

— The practice of "Opening Up Your Energy Centers" was given to me by Sky Canyon. He in turn got it from Ram Dass during a retreat at the Lama Foundation in Taos, New Mexico.

— The relaxation technique in the "Creative Meditation" section came from a course called Silva Mind Control; they're now called Silva Mind Body Healing. They teach courses nationally, and they are excellent.

— Tarthang Tulku taught me about our three bodies as described in "Meditations on Our Three Bodies." I studied *kum nye* (Tibetan massage and yoga) from him, also, at the Nyingma Meditation Center in Berkeley. Paul Clemens, the editor of the first edition of this work and a dharma brother, added the bit about rubbing the earlobes.

— The practice called "Closing the Gates" was given to me by my first teacher of yoga and meditation, Professor Arya, from the University of Minnesota.

— The last chant in "Mantras" is freely adapted from a prayer of protection given by Catherine Ponder in one of her many books.

11 Aging and Healing

— The pattern of running energy in "Create a Healthy, Beautiful Body" was adapted from *The Art of True Healing* by Israel Regardie.

— Many of the ideas in "The Principles of Healing" section were inspired by the healer Mildred Jackson, who taught classes for many years in Albany, California.

13 Enlightenment

— Tarthang Tulku told me the story of the woman dreaming about losing her head.

Addendum

— Much of this material came from Tarthang Tulku's stories. Other parts of the story came from various books, especially from Yeshe Tsogyal's biography of Padma Sambhava that is included in *The Tibetan Book of the Great Liberation*, translated by W. Y. Evans-Wentz and published by Oxford.

Suggested Reading

The Art of True Healing: The Unlimited Power of Prayer and Visualization by Israel Regardie. Filled with practices that are easy to do, including a powerful meditation, the Middle Pillar meditation, that can heal our bodies and help us improve our lives in every way imaginable.

As You Think by James Allen. This is certainly one of the greatest self-improvement — or rather, self-*empowerment* — books ever written. It's worth reading or listening to on audio repeatedly. Here's one of my favorite passages from the book, words I've had up on my wall in big letters for years:

"You will become as great as your dominant aspiration.... If you cherish a vision, a lofty ideal in your heart, you will realize it."

Creative Visualization: Use the Power of Your Imagination to Create What You Want in Your Life by Shakti Gawain. This book should be taught in our high schools. It's a classic.

The Magical Path: Creating the Life of Your Dreams and a World That Works for All by Marc Allen. Writers can never judge their own work objectively, but this book is the one I would most highly recommend to almost anyone at the moment. Filled with simple practices and processes that can have great results.

The Power of Partnership: Seven Relationships That Will Change Your Life by Riane Eisler. This book is the operating manual for living well. It describes how to weed out all our fear-based activities — including the need to control others and domination and exploitation in any form — and how to base all our thoughts and actions on love and respect, creating win-win relationships with all. There is hope for the world. The book shows us how to work together and create a sustainable world that works for us all.

The Power of Now: A Guide to Spiritual Enlightenment by Eckhart Tolle. The single best book I've ever read. I'll include part of a blog post I wrote about it a few years ago:

> Books are very powerful. They have changed people's lives ever since they were invented; they have changed the world.

> *The Power of Now* is the single most powerfully life-changing book I've ever found. I've spent a large part of my lifetime trying to discover the wisdom of the ages and translate it into words I could understand and realize in my life.

And that's exactly what Eckhart Tolle has done in *The Power of Now*: it's a translation of the most brilliant, deepest teachings of all great traditions, East and West and indigenous and everything else, into words we can understand in a way that affects every moment of our lives. It is the greatest book I've ever read (or published).

I haven't been able to finish it yet. (I told that to Eckhart — he thought it was funny.) I have to read it very slowly, because a phrase keeps stopping me, and I have to think about it. It's not a book to read straight through; it's a very precious thing, and if we are to receive its gifts, we have to stop and ponder and sit with the words and see how they impact our life experience.

I slowly read through the book until I came to page 155 (in the hardcover edition), where a phrase stopped me that I reflected on for the next eighteen months or so:

"To offer no resistance to life is to be in a state of grace, ease, and lightness."

That's it in a nutshell.

Now, after reading the book for over a decade, I've only gotten to the next page (page 156), because I came to a phrase that sums up everything I need to know for the rest of my life. If I remember these words, I can live and die in peace:

> **"The happiness that is derived**
> **from some secondary source is never very deep.**
> **It is only a pale reflection of the joy of Being,**
> **the vibrant peace that you find within**
> **as you enter a state of nonresistance.**

> **"Being takes you beyond the polar opposites of the mind**
> **and frees you from dependency on form.**
> **Even if everything were to collapse**
> **and crumble around you, you would still feel**
> **a deep inner core of peace.**

> **"You may not be happy, but you will be at peace."**

Nothing more needs to be said.

About the Author

Marc Allen is an internationally renowned author, speaker, and composer. His books, online courses, and seminars have been life-changing experiences for many people.

He cofounded New World Library (with Shakti Gawain) in 1977, and has guided the company from a small start-up to its current position as one of the leading independent publishers in the country. He has published several books, including *The Magical Path*, *The Greatest Secret of All*, *The Millionaire Course*, and *Visionary Business*. His audio projects include *Success With Ease: Creating the Life of Your Dreams* and *Stress Reduction and Creative Meditations*.

He is also an accomplished composer and musician, and has produced several albums of music. For more information about Marc Allen and his seminars and teleconferences, go to www.MarcAllen.com. For more on his publishing company, go to www.NewWorldLibrary.com. To sample his music, go to www.WaterCourseMedia.com.

NEW WORLD LIBRARY is dedicated to publishing books and other media that inspire and challenge us to improve the quality of our lives and the world.

We are a socially and environmentally aware company. We recognize that we have an ethical responsibility to our customers, our staff members, and our planet.

We serve our customers by creating the finest publications possible on personal growth, creativity, spirituality, wellness, and other areas of emerging importance. We serve New World Library employees with generous benefits, significant profit sharing, and constant encouragement to pursue their most expansive dreams.

As a member of the Green Press Initiative, we print an increasing number of books with soy-based ink on 100 percent postconsumer-waste recycled paper. Also, we power our offices with solar energy and contribute to nonprofit organizations working to make the world a better place for us all.

Our products are available in bookstores everywhere.

www.newworldlibrary.com

At NewWorldLibrary.com you can download our catalog,
subscribe to our e-newsletter, read our blog,
and link to authors' websites, videos, and podcasts.

Find us on Facebook, follow us on Twitter, and watch us on
YouTube.

Send your questions and comments our way!
You make it possible for us to do what we love to do.

Phone: 415-884-2100 or 800-972-6657
Catalog requests: Ext. 10 | Orders: Ext. 52
Fax: 415-884-2199
escort@newworldlibrary.com
14 Pamaron Way, Novato, CA 94949